Power Maths

Year 4
Textbook 4C

White Rose Maths Edition

Ash

Ash is curious.
He likes to help if you get stuck.

helpful

flexible

brave

determined

Sparks

Flo

Astrid

Dexter

Series editor: Tony Staneff
Lead author: Josh Lury

Consultants (first edition): Professor Liu Jian and Professor Zhang Dan

Author team (first edition): David Board, Tim Handley, Derek Huby, Timothy Weal, Paul Wrangles and White Rose Maths (Emily Fox, Jilly Todd and Rachel Webster)

How to use this book

These pages make sure we're ready for the unit ahead. Find out what we'll be learning and brush up on your skills.

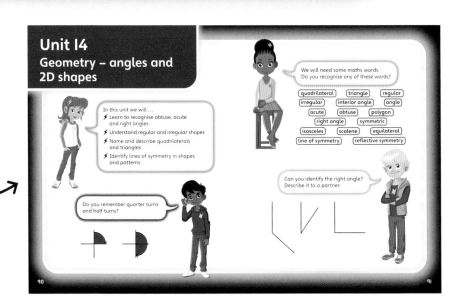

Discover

Lessons start with **Discover**.

Here, we explore new maths problems.

Can you work out how to find the answer?

Don't be afraid to make mistakes. Learn from them and try again!

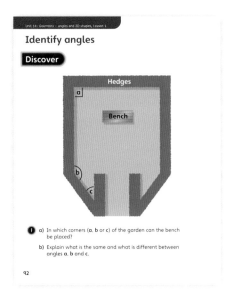

Share

Next, we share our ideas with the class.

Did we all solve the problems the same way?
What ideas can you try?

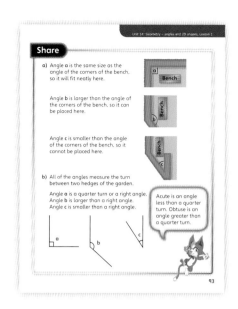

Think together

Then we have a go at some more problems together. Use what you have just learnt to help you.

We'll try a challenge too!

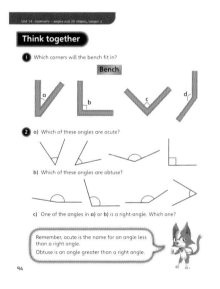

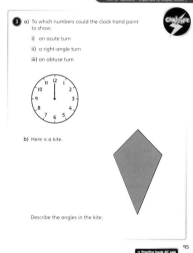

This tells you which page to go to in your **Practice Book**.

At the end of each unit there's an **End of unit check**. This is our chance to show how much we have learnt.

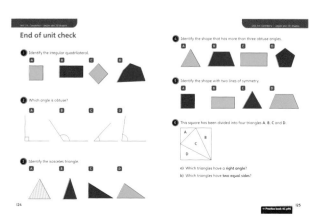

Unit 11
Decimals ❷

In this unit we will …

⚡ Work out what we need to make a whole

⚡ Write and partition decimals

⚡ Compare and order decimals

⚡ Round decimals to the nearest whole number

⚡ Learn the decimal equivalents of fractions such as $\frac{1}{2}$, $\frac{1}{4}$ and $\frac{3}{4}$

In the last unit, we learnt how to show a decimal.

What decimal is shown here?

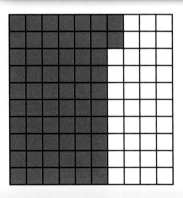

We will need some maths words.
How many of these can you remember?

tenths   hundredths   0·1 and 0·01
equivalent   whole number   round
greater than (>)   less than (<)   equal to (=)
order   compare   decimal place
ascending   descending

We will also need to know where to find
a decimal on a number line. This will
help us round the number.

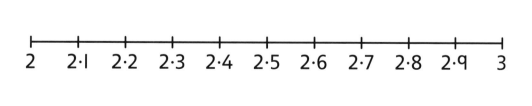

2   2·1   2·2   2·3   2·4   2·5   2·6   2·7   2·8   2·9   3

Make a whole

Discover

Jamie

Alex

Strawberry
Jam Recipe:

1 kg strawberries
$\frac{1}{2}$ kg sugar
4 lemons

0·7 kg

0·46 kg

1 Jamie and Alex both want to make strawberry jam.

a) How many more kilograms of strawberries does Jamie need?

b) How many more kilograms of strawberries does Alex need?

8

Share

a) I whole kilogram of strawberries is needed to make the jam.

The number 0·7 is made up of 7 tenths.

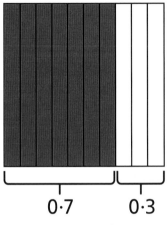

0·7   0·3

I used a diagram to help me. I know what $\frac{7}{10}$ looks like.

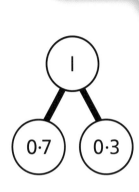

3 more tenths are needed to make I whole.

3 tenths = 0·3

Jamie needs another 0·3 kg of strawberries.

b) The number 0·46 is made up of 46 hundredths.

Another 54 hundredths are needed to make I whole.

54 hundredths = 0·54

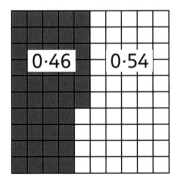

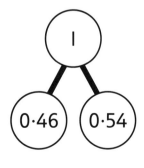

I did not count each hundredth needed to make a whole. I noticed that 46 and 54 are a number bond to 100.

Alex needs another 0·54 kg of strawberries.

Think together

1 Use the models to complete the calculations.

a) 0·6 + 0·⬜ = 1

b) 0·8 + 0·⬜ = 1

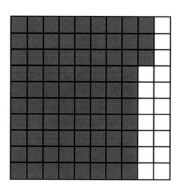

c) 0·83 + 0·⬜⬜ = 1

2 Complete the part-whole models.

a)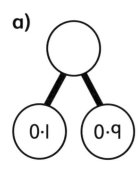

b)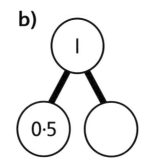

c)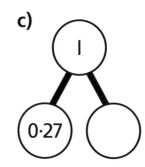

d)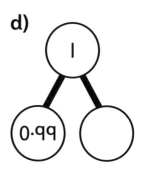

3 Jamilla, Luis and Andy want to fill a jug with 1 litre of water.

a) Jamilla has two cups with different amounts of water in each.

She pours the water into the jug. How much more water will she need to fill the jug?

b) Luis has two cups.

He pours the water into the jug. How much more water will Luis need to fill the jug?

> I will use a hundredths grid with different colours to represent the cups to help me.

c) Andy has already poured the water from two cups into his jug.

His jug is now full with 1 litre of water.

How much water could have been in each of his cups?

> I wonder if I can find more than one answer.

11

→ **Practice book 4C p6**

Partition decimals

Discover

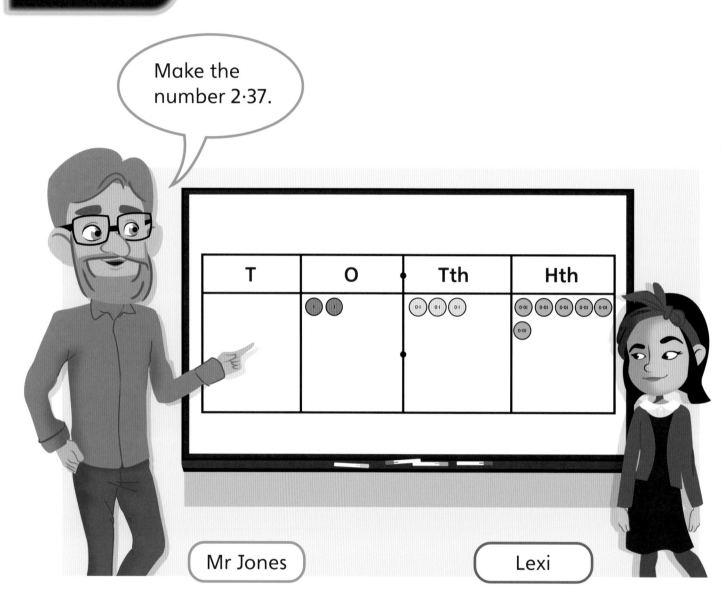

Make the number 2·37.

Mr Jones

Lexi

1 **a)** What mistake has Lexi made?

b) Partition 2·37 using a part-whole model.

Write this as an addition.

Share

a) Lexi's answer shows 2 ones and 3 tenths, so this is correct.

> I looked carefully at each digit in the decimal number.

> Remember, the first digit after a decimal point shows tenths. The second digit after a decimal point shows hundredths.

Lexi's hundredths column only has 6 hundredths.

T	O		Tth	Hth
	⚫⚫		0·1 0·1 0·1	0·01 0·01 0·01 0·01 0·01 0·01
	2	•	3	6

2·37 has 7 hundredths, so this is Lexi's mistake.

This is the correct place value grid.

T	O		Tth	Hth
	⚫⚫		0·1 0·1 0·1	0·01 0·01 0·01 0·01 0·01 0·01 0·01
	2	•	3	7

b) 2·37 = 2 + 0·3 + 0·07

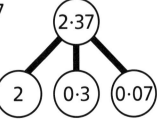

Think together

1 Work out the missing numbers.

T	O		Tth	Hth
	●●●●●		0·1 0·1 0·1 0·1	0·01 0·01 0·01 0·01 0·01 / 0·01 0·01 0·01 0·01

a) 5·49 is equal to ☐ ones, ☐ tenths and ☐ hundredths.

5·49 = 5 + 0·☐ + 0·0☐

b) Make the number 0·26 on a place value grid.

O		Tth	Hth

0·26 is equal to ☐ ones ☐ tenths and ☐ hundredths.

0·26 = ☐ + ☐

2 Complete the part-whole models.

a)

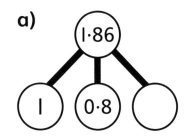

b)

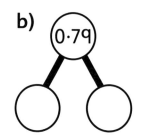

c)

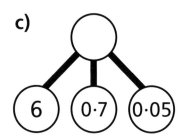

14

 3 Ebo has used five counters to make the number 20·12.

T	O		Tth	Hth
⬤⬤		⬤		⬤⬤

How many different numbers can you make using the same place value grid and five counters?

T	O		Tth	Hth

I will draw a part-whole model for each number.

I wonder how many numbers will have just one **decimal place**.

One decimal place means just one digit after the decimal point.

15

→ **Practice book 4C p9**

Flexibly partition decimals

Discover

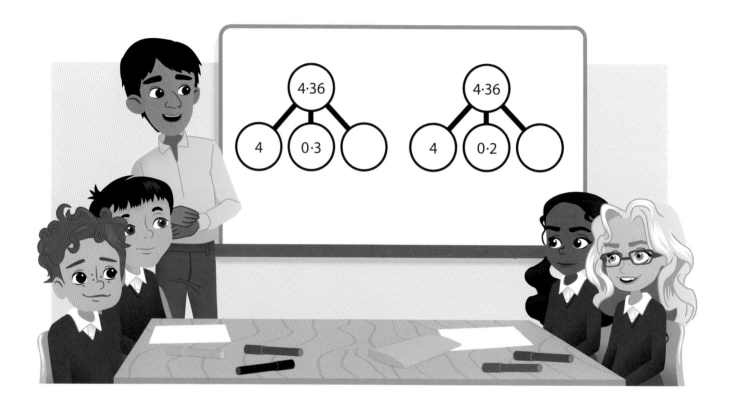

1 **a)** Make the number 4·36 from place value counters.

b) Complete the part-whole models.

Share

a) 4·36 is 4 ones, 3 tenths and 6 hundredths.

T	O	•	Tth	Hth
		•		
	4	•	3	6

b)

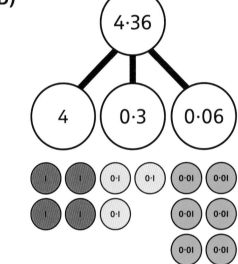

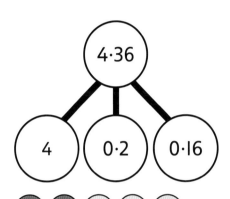
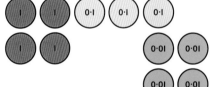

I lined the place value counters up underneath the parts and worked out what I had left.

17

Think together

1 Here is 0·45 in place value counters.

T	O	•	Tth	Hth
		•	0·1 0·1 0·1 0·1	0·01 0·01 0·01 0·01 0·01
		•	4	5

Complete the partitions.

a)

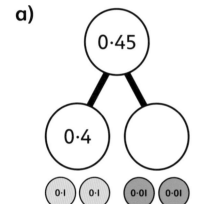

c)

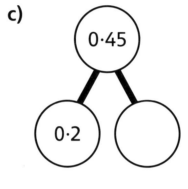

b)

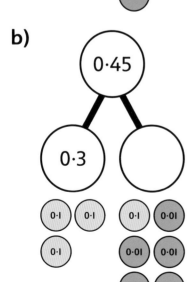

2 Partition 5·26 in four different ways.

T	O		Tth	Hth
	① ① ① ① ①		⓪·¹ ⓪·¹	⓪·⁰¹ ⓪·⁰¹ ⓪·⁰¹ ⓪·⁰¹ ⓪·⁰¹ ⓪·⁰¹
	5		2	6

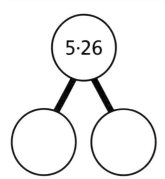

3 Complete the partitions.

Set A

0·89 = 0·8 + ☐

0·89 = 0·7 + ☐

0·89 = 0·6 + ☐

0·89 = 0·4 + ☐

0·89 = 0·1 + ☐

Set B

3·42 = 3 + 0·4 + ☐

3·42 = 3 + 0·3 + ☐

3·42 = 3 + 0·2 + ☐

3·42 = 3 + ☐

3·42 = 2 + ☐ + 0·02

I will draw part-whole models to help me.

19

Compare decimals

Discover

I think my sunflower is the tallest.

No, mine is the tallest!

0·67 m

0·76 m

Bella

Zac

1 **a)** Who is correct, Bella or Zac? Work out whether to use a < or > sign in the box.

0·67 m ◯ 0·76 m

b) Another sunflower is 0·79 m tall. Zac thinks this sunflower is taller than his sunflower.

Is Zac correct? How do you know?

20

Share

a) The numbers 0·67 and 0·76 both have 0 ones.

O		Tth	Hth
	•	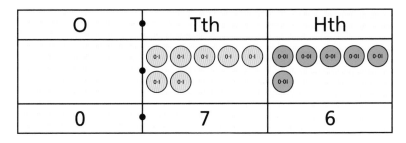	
0	•	6	7

O		Tth	Hth
	•		
0	•	7	6

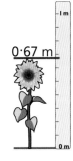

0·67 m

0·76 m

0·67 has 6 tenths and 0·76 has 7 tenths.

So, 0·76 is the largest number.
Zac is correct.

0·67 m < 0·76 m

< means less than or fewer than.
> means greater than.

----

b) Zac's sunflower is 0·76 m tall.

0·76 = 7 tenths + 6 hundredths
0·79 = 7 tenths + 9 hundredths

0·79 has more hundredths than 0·76.
So, 0·79 is greater than 0·76.
Zac is correct.

I put the numbers in a place value grid. To compare the numbers, I started by looking at the tenths.

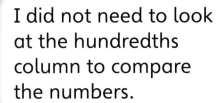

I did not need to look at the hundredths column to compare the numbers.

I looked at the hundredths to compare the numbers.

Think together

1 In each pair, which number is bigger?

a)
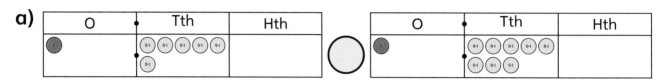

b)
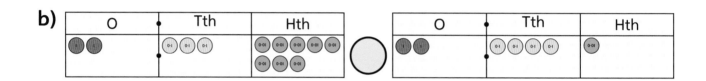

c)
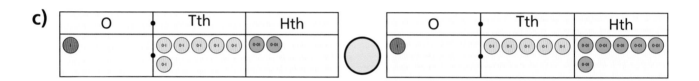

2 Complete these statements using < or > signs.

a) 0·68 ◯ 0·65

b) 0·38 ◯ 0·45

c) 2·08 ◯ 3·24

d) 16·81 ◯ 6·79

3 Holly and Jen are competing in the long jump.

They have three attempts each.

Attempt	Distance Jen jumped	Distance Holly jumped
1	2·4 m	2·7 m
2	2·36 m	2·48 m
3	1·95 m	2·10 m

a) Who jumps further each time?

b) Make 2·4 and 2·7 using place value counters.

c) Complete the statement. 2·4 ◯ 2·7

23

→ Practice book 4C p15

Order decimals

1 **a)** Order the rabbits from the lightest to the heaviest.

   b) A fourth rabbit, Flopsy, is weighed.

   Flopsy is the second heaviest out of the four rabbits.

   What might Flopsy's mass be?

Share

I put the numbers into a place value grid. To order the numbers, I started by looking at the largest place value.

a)

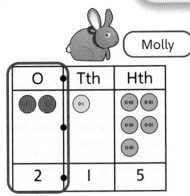

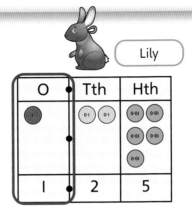

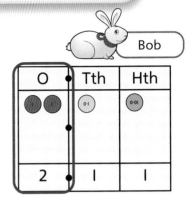

1·25 has 1 one and the others have 2 ones, so Lily is the lightest rabbit.

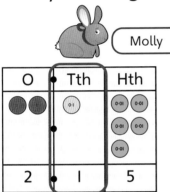

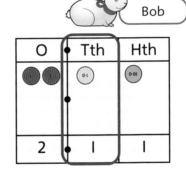

Next, I compared the tenths. Both 2·15 and 2·11 have 1 tenth.

So then I compared the hundredths.

2·15 has 5 hundredths.
2·11 has 1 hundredth.
So 2·15 is the largest number.
Lily is the lightest, Bob is second lightest and Molly is the heaviest.

Lightest ⟶ Heaviest

| Lily | Bob | Molly |
| 1·25 kg | 2·11 kg | 2·15 kg |

b) Flopsy's mass is between Bob's and Molly's, so between 2·11 kg and 2·15 kg.

Her mass must have hundredths that are bigger than 1 but smaller than 5. Flopsy's mass could be 2·12 kg, 2·13 kg or 2·14 kg.

Think together

1 Order the numbers from smallest to greatest.

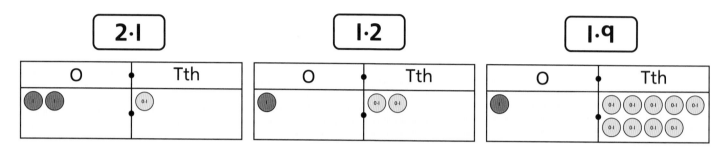

2 Put each set of numbers in order from smallest to greatest.

a) 1·43 2·33 1·53

b) 25·31 15·62 19·07

I will put the numbers in place value grids to help me.

 a) The number cards below are ordered from greatest to smallest.

One of the numbers is in the wrong place.

| 9·46 | 9·34 | 9·82 | 9·28 | 9·08 |

Which number is in the wrong place?

b) What digits could go in each box so the numbers are in ascending order?

5·3☐,   5·☐3,   ☐·54,   6·☐9

I wonder if there is more than one answer.

Ascending means from smallest to greatest.

Round to the nearest whole

Discover

The amount of sugar is closer to 7 grams than 6 grams.

Mo

If I round to the nearest whole number, there is I gram of salt.

Amount per 40 g serving (without milk)

Fat	Saturates	Sugar	Sa
0·7 g	0·2 g	6·8 g	

1 **a)** Round the amount of sugar to the nearest whole number.

Is Mo correct?

b) What is the smallest possible amount of salt to I decimal place?

Share

a) There are 6·8 g of sugar in a portion of the cereal.

I drew a number line going up in tenths to help me round the number.

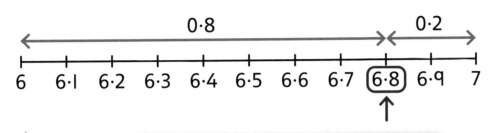

Look at the tenths. If there are 5 or more tenths, then we round up to the next whole number.

8 tenths is '5 or more', so 6·8 rounded to the nearest whole number is 7.

Mo is correct. The amount of sugar is closer to 7 g than 6 g.

b)

To find the smallest possible amount of salt, look at the numbers below 1.

To round to the nearest whole number, look at the tenths that are 5 or more.

The smallest possible amount of salt is 0·5 g.

I know 1 is between 0 and 2.

I drew a different number line to help me decide.

Think together

Look at the tenths. If there are 4 or fewer tenths, then we round down to the last whole number.

1 Round each number to the nearest whole number.

a) 4·2

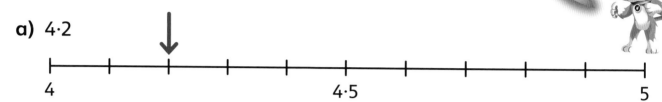

b) 5·6

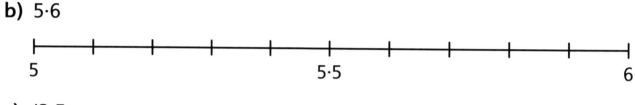

c) 12·5

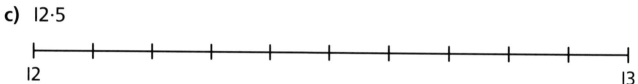

2 Work out the previous and next whole number and then round each number to the nearest whole number.

Previous whole number		Next whole number
☐	3·2	☐
Previous whole number		Next whole number
☐	4·5	☐
Previous whole number		Next whole number
☐	0·7	☐
Previous whole number		Next whole number
☐	11·8	☐

CHALLENGE

3 **a)**

If I round all these numbers to the nearest whole number, they all round to 8.

Jamilla

| 7·5 | | 8·5 | | 8·1 | | 7·7 | | 7·9 |

Is Jamilla correct? Explain your answer.

7   8   9

I will look at the number of tenths to help me round the numbers.

b) Write down four other numbers that round to 8 to the nearest whole number.

→ **Practice book 4C p21**

Halves and quarters as decimals

Discover

There are 0·5 litres of orange juice in this jug. 0·5 is the same as $\frac{1}{2}$.

Ebo

Amelia

I Ebo's jug is $\frac{1}{2}$ full. Amelia's jug is $\frac{3}{4}$ full.

   a) Is Ebo correct, that 0·5 is equivalent to $\frac{1}{2}$? Explain your answer.

   b) What is $\frac{3}{4}$ as a decimal?

Share

a) Ebo's jug is $\frac{1}{2}$ full.

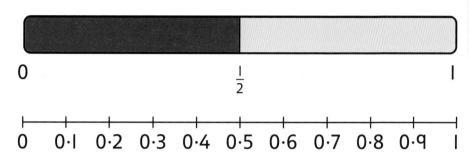

> I remembered where $\frac{1}{2}$ is on a number line. I know that $\frac{1}{2}$ means I out of 2 equal parts.

We can see that $\frac{1}{2}$ is equivalent to 0·5, so Ebo is correct.

b) Amelia's jug is $\frac{3}{4}$ full.

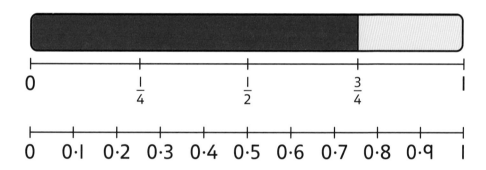

$\frac{3}{4}$ is exactly half-way between 0·7 and 0·8.

So, $\frac{3}{4}$ is equivalent to 0·75.

> I did it a different way. I shaded $\frac{3}{4}$ of the 100 squares on a hundredths grid. That is 75 squares. Each square is equal to I hundredth.

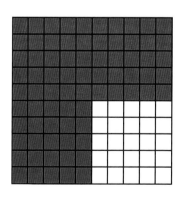

75 hundredths = 0·75

So, $\frac{3}{4}$ as a decimal is 0·75.

33

Think together

1 Write $\frac{1}{4}$ as a decimal.

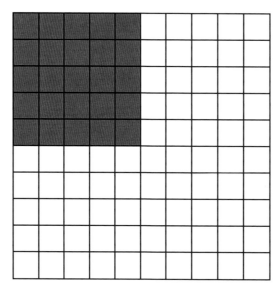

2 Discuss with a partner how you could use the diagram to show $\frac{1}{2}$ as a decimal.

$\frac{1}{2}$ is equivalent to ⬚ hundredths.

$\frac{1}{2}$ is equivalent to ⬚ tenths.

$\frac{1}{2} = 0 \cdot$ ⬚

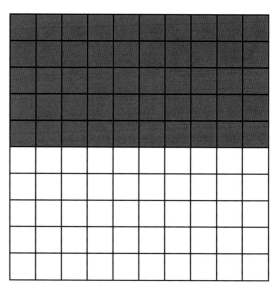

3 **a)** Which of these does not show $\frac{3}{4}$?

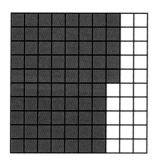

0·75

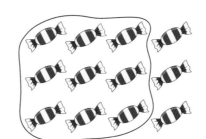

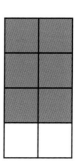

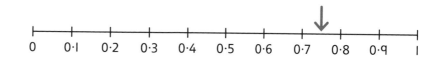

3·4

I think it would help to write a decimal or a fraction for each diagram. Then I could use my knowledge of equivalent fractions and decimals.

b) Write these fractions as decimals.

$1\frac{1}{4}$ $1\frac{1}{2}$ $1\frac{3}{4}$

35

→ **Practice book 4C p24**

End of unit check

1 Which number completes the calculation?

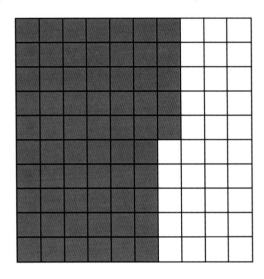

$$0.65 + \boxed{} = 1$$

| A | 1·65 | B | 0·66 | C | 0·45 | D | 0·35 |

2 Which of the following is equal to 2 ones, 5 tenths and 3 hundredths?

| A | 253 | B | 352 | C | 2·53 | D | 25·3 |

3 What number is missing from the part-whole model?

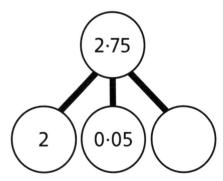

| A | 7 | B | 0·7 | C | 0·07 | D | 27 |

4 These numbers are listed in order from the smallest to greatest. What is the missing digit?

| 3·46 | 3·79 | 4·28 | 4·2? | 4·38 |

A 7   **B** 0   **C** 9   **D** 3

5 Which of the following numbers does not round to 6 when rounded to the nearest whole number?

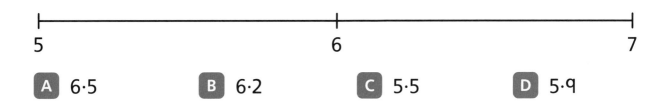

5   6   7

A 6·5   **B** 6·2   **C** 5·5   **D** 5·9

6 Complete the table.

Fraction	Decimal
$\frac{1}{4}$	
	0·5
	0·75
$1\frac{1}{2}$	
$1\frac{3}{4}$	
	2·5
	3·25

→ Practice book 4C p27

Unit 12
Money

In this unit we will ...

⚡ Write money in pounds and pence, using a decimal point

⚡ Order, add and subtract amounts of money

⚡ Make estimates with money

⚡ Find change

⚡ Solve simple word problems involving money

Do you know how to work out how much money there is? Remember to add the pounds first and then the pence.

We will need some maths words. Do you know what they all mean?

notes   coins   pounds (£)   pence (p)

add   subtract   change

total   order

greater than (>)   less than (<)

cheaper   more expensive   estimate

over estimate   under estimate

We need to be able to add and subtract using column methods.

56p + 89p

56p + 89p = 145p

145p = £1 and 45p

	H	T	O
		5	6
+		8	9
	1	4	5
	1	1	

Write money using decimals

Discover

1 **a)** How much money does Emma have?

b) How much money does Danny have?

Key 1p 2p 5p 10p 20p 50p £1 £2

Share

a) Emma has 100 1p coins.

This is 100p, which is £1·00.

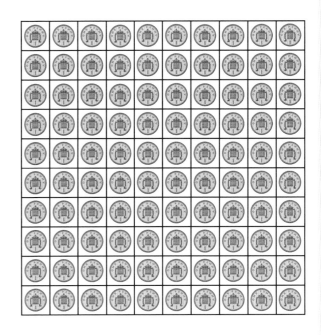

Money is usually written as a decimal for pounds and pence.

We write two 0s after the decimal point to show that there are 0 pence.

b)

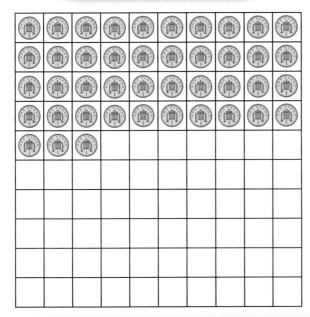

Danny has 43 1p coins.

This is $\frac{43}{100}$.

$\frac{43}{100} = 0·43$.

Danny has £0·43.

Remember, the decimal point separates the pounds from the pence.

I worked out what fraction of Danny's 100 square is filled with 1p coins. Then I converted this to a decimal.

Think together

1 How much money is shown on each 100 square?

Write each amount as a decimal with a pound sign.

a)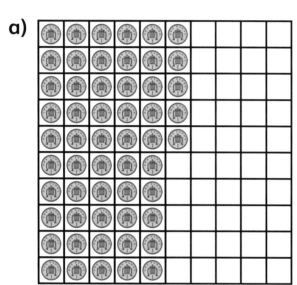

b)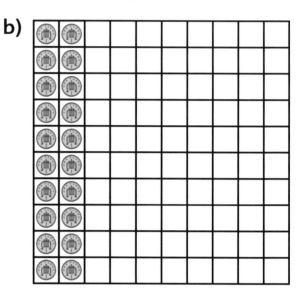

2 How much money in pounds is there in each box?

A

C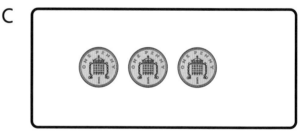

B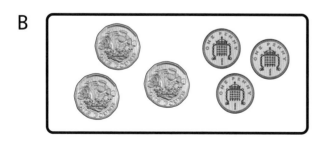

D

Key 1p 2p 5p 10p 20p 50p £1 £2

 **£0·50**

 **£2·30**

 CHALLENGE

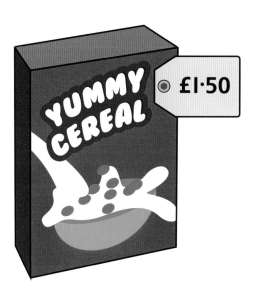 **£1·50**

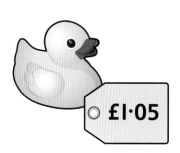 **£1·05**

Choose from the coins below to make the correct amount for each item.

I will try to find more than one way to make each amount.

 £5 £10  £20 £50

43

→ Practice book 4C p29

Convert between pounds and pence

Discover

1 a) How much money does Bella have in pence?

b) How much money does Bella have in pounds and pence?

44

Key 1p 2p 5p 10p 20p 50p £1 £2

Share

a) 100p + 100p + 36p = 236p

Bella has 236p in total.

 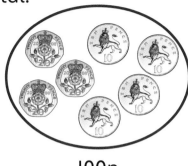 

100p	100p	36p

b) 100p is equal to £1.

Bella has £2·36 in total.

 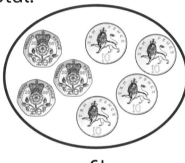 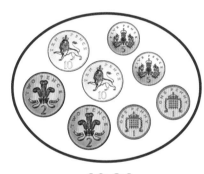

£1	£1	£0·36

Remember, we use a decimal point to separate the whole pounds from the pence.

 £5   £10   £20 £50

Think together

1 Write the total amount in pence.

a)

b) Now convert the amount into pounds and write it as a decimal.

2 Convert each amount into pounds and write them as decimals.

 150p

 303p

 299p

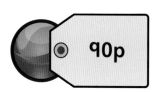 90p

Key 1p 2p 5p 10p 20p 50p £1 £2

3 **a)** Write the value of each coin or note in pounds, as a decimal.

b) Who is correct, Dexter or Astrid?

I wrote £0·1 for the 1p coin.

I wrote £0·1 for the 10p coin.

 £5   £10    £20   £50

→ **Practice book 4C p32**

Compare amounts of money

Discover

Isla

1 **a)** Which is more expensive, the football or the colouring pencils?

b) Which items could Isla buy with the money she has?

48

Key 1p 2p 5p 10p 20p 50p £1 £2

Share

a)

I think the pencils are more expensive, because 75 is greater than 5.

I don't think that's right. I converted them both to pence.

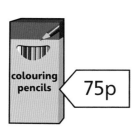
colouring pencils
75p

75 < 500

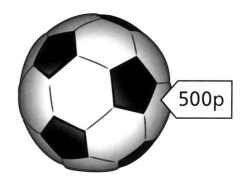
500p

The football is more expensive than the colouring pencils.

b) Isla has a £5 note.

Isla could buy any items that cost £5·00 or 500p or less.

£5

colouring pencils
75p

NOTEPAD
£0·50

So she could buy the football, because that is exactly £5, or she could buy the colouring pencils and the notepad.

 £5 £10 £20 £50

Think together

1

| 59 pence | £5·99 | £0·99 | 9 pounds 95 pence | 595p |

59 pence

↓

| 0 | £1 | £2 | £3 | £4 | £5 | £6 | £7 | £8 | £9 | £10 |

a) What is the cheapest item?

b) What is the most expensive item?

c) Order the items from the least to the most expensive.

2 Alex has these coins.

Which of the toys from Question I could Alex buy?

Key 1p 2p 5p 10p 20p 50p £1 £2

CHALLENGE

Kate

Amelia

Richard

Max

Kate, Amelia, Richard and Max are comparing how much money they have.

Max: I have the most money as I have a £5 note.

Richard: No, I have the most money as I have the greatest number of coins.

What mistakes have Max and Richard made?

I will put the numbers in ascending order and see if either of them are correct.

I think one of them might be right, but it is not for the reason that they say.

 £5   £10   £20   £50

→ Practice book 4C p35

Estimate with money

Discover

Let's try to work out an estimate for the total cost of what we need.

Eggs £2·99

Cereal £1·99

Milk 99p

Toshi

Jen

1 **a)** What is the same and what is different about the price of each item?

b) Estimate the total cost.

Key 1p 2p 5p 10p 20p 50p £1 £2

Share

a)

I made a table to make it easier to compare the amounts of money.

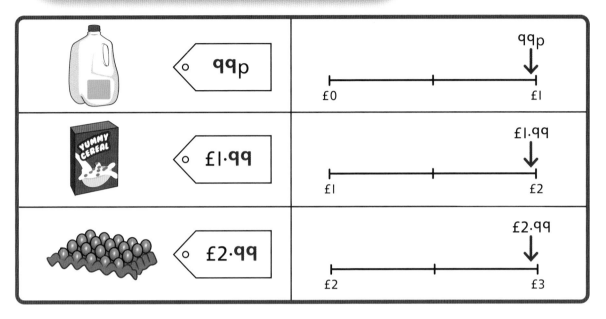

Each item has 99p in the pence part of the price.

But they all have different numbers of pounds in the pounds part of the price.

b) To make an estimate, find the nearest whole pound for each item.

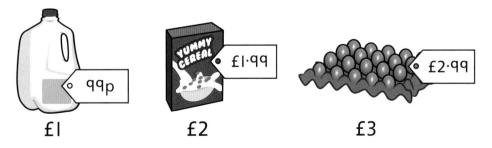

£1 + £2 + £3 = £6
A good estimate is £6.

Think together

1 Which items cost approximately £5?

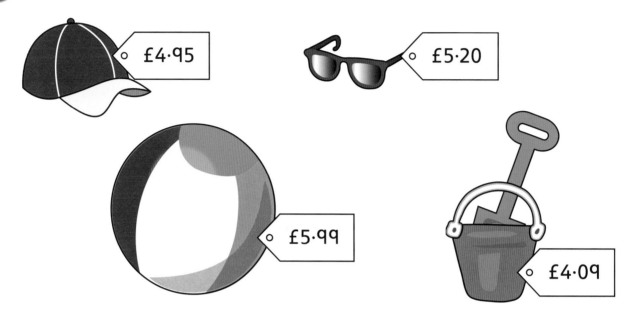

£4·95

£5·20

£5·99

£4·09

2 Write a suitable estimate for the cost of each item.

£0·49

£18·75

£51·25

£47·50

Key lp 2p 5p 10p 20p 50p £l £2

3 Here are some more items that Toshi and Jen want to buy.

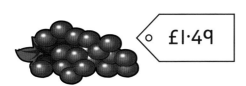 £1·49  £3·95  £2·49

a) Estimate the total cost.

I wonder if I always need to estimate to a whole pound.

An **over estimate** is where it is more than the actual total. An **under estimate** is where it is less than the actual total.

b) Do you think your estimate is an under or an over estimate?

 £5  £10   £20   £50

→ **Practice book 4C p38**

Calculate with money

Discover

Alex   Holly   Jamie

1 **a)** Alex buys the Fast Track DVD and a T-shirt.

Work out the total cost.

b) She pays with a £5 note.

Work out how much change she gets.

Key 1p 2p 5p 10p 20p 50p £1 £2

Share

a)

I converted the prices to pence, then used a column method to add the amounts.

	H	T	O
	3	3	5
+		9	0
	4	2	5
	1		

The total cost is 425p.

This is the same as £4·25.

b) To find how much change Alex gets, count on from £4·25 to £5·00.

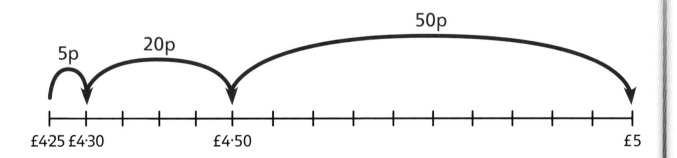

5p + 20p + 50p = 75p

Alex will get 75p change.

 £5  £10 £20 £50

Think together

1 **a)** What is the total cost of these items?

£1·60   £3·35

b) What is the total cost of these items?

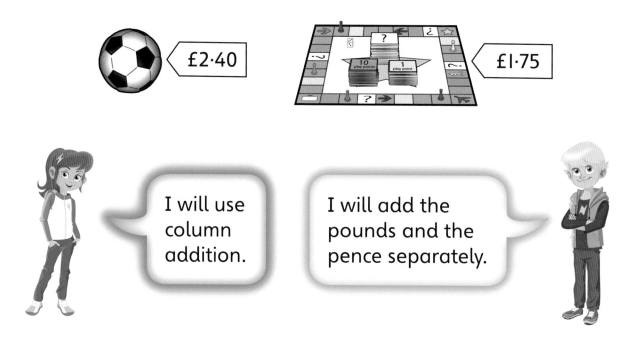

£2·40   £1·75

I will use column addition.

I will add the pounds and the pence separately.

2 Zac spends £2·35. He pays with a £10 note.

How much change will he receive?

£2·35

£0   £1   £2   £3   £4   £5   £6   £7   £8   £9   £10

Key 1p 2p 5p 10p 20p 50p £1 £2

3

CHALLENGE

Ambika

Bella

Ambika spends £2·68.
She pays with a £5 note.
How much change does
Ambika receive?

Bella buys some items.
She pays with a £5 note.
She gets £3·46 change.
How much does she spend?

What is the same and what is different about the two questions?

I think the methods are
similar, but the questions
are not the same.

I am going to draw a
bar model to help me
work out the answer to
each question.

 £5   £10   £20   £50

→ Practice book 4C p41

Solve problems with money

Discover

I a) Kate wants to buy 3 buns at the cheapest price.

Should she buy a pack of buns for £1·50 or 3 single buns for 65p each?

b) Max buys I pack of 6 buns for £3·50.

Is this the best deal?

60   Key Ip 2p 5p I0p  20p 50p £I £2

Share

a) An individual bun costs 65p.

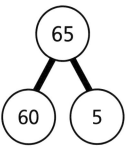

I worked out the cost of 3 single buns by multiplying.

3 × 60p = 180p

3 × 5p = 15p

I worked out the cost of 1 bun in a pack by dividing 150p by 3. This was 50p per bun, which is **cheaper** than 65p.

180p + 15p = 195p = £1·95

A bag of 3 buns costs £1·50.

£1·95 > £1·50 so it is cheaper for Kate to buy the pack of 3 buns.

b) Max could have bought 6 single buns instead of a pack of 6 buns.

6 × 60p = 360p

6 × 5p = 30p

6 × 65p = 390p

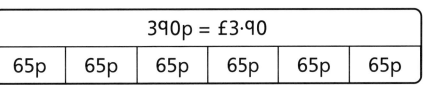

390p = £3·90					
65p	65p	65p	65p	65p	65p

Or Max could have bought 2 packs of 3 buns.

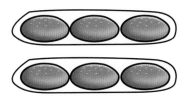

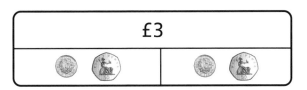

The cost of 2 packs of 3 buns is £3. This is cheaper than both £3·50 and £3·90.

Max could have got a better deal.

 £5 £10 £20 £50

Think together

1 Kate has 3 goes on the hook-a-duck stall.

How much change does she get from £5?

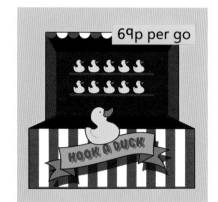

69p per go

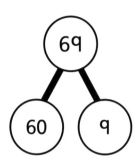

$3 \times 60p = \boxed{}p$

$3 \times 9p = \boxed{}p$

$3 \times 69p = \boxed{}p$

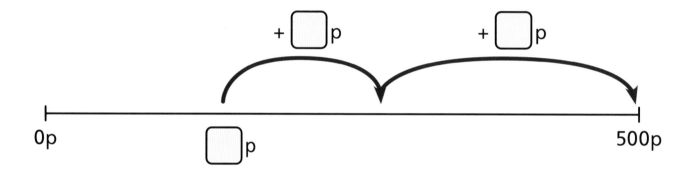

$+ \boxed{}p \qquad + \boxed{}p$

0p $\boxed{}p$ 500p

Kate receives £$\boxed{}$ change from £5.

2 Bella buys 10 raffle tickets.

She gets £6·50 change from £10.

a) How much did Bella spend on raffle tickets?

b) How much does each raffle ticket cost?

Key 1p 2p 5p 10p 20p 50p £1 £2

3

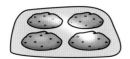

Deal 1:
bag of 4 cookies
for £2·40

Deal 2:
bag of 6 cookies
for £3·36

I think the bag of 4
cookies is the best deal.

Lee

Is Lee correct?

Explain your method.

I will work out the cost of
1 cookie from each bag.

I will work out the cost of
12 cookies from each bag.

 £5   £10   £20  £50

63

→ **Practice book 4C p44**

End of unit check

1 How much money is shown here?

| | A £10 | | B £71 | | C £3·67 | | D £4·67 |

2 What is this amount in pounds?

| | A £3 | | B £0·30 | | C £0·3 | | D £0·03 |

3 Which item is the most expensive?

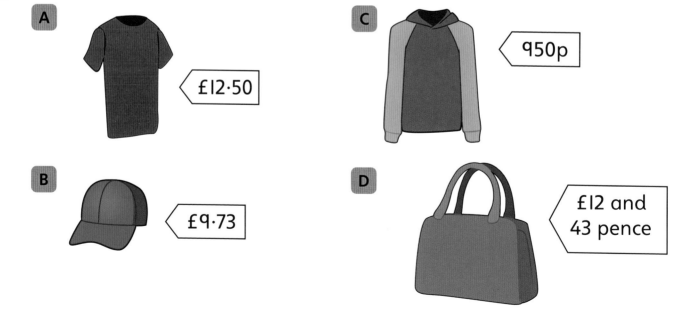

A £12·50

B £9·73

C 950p

D £12 and 43 pence

Key 1p 2p 5p 10p 20p 50p £1 £2

4 Adam buys a cup of tea with a £5 note.

He receives £3·15 change.

How much did the cup of tea cost?

A £1·85   **B** £2·15   **C** £2·85   **D** £3·15

5 Which of the following amounts does not give an estimate of £8?

A £7·50   **B** £7·90   **C** £8·04   **D** £8·50

6 What do you get if you add together £1·34 and 72p?

A £1·96   **B** £2·06   **C** £73·34   **D** You cannot add them together.

7 A pencil costs 17p.

Max buys 9 pencils for his friends.

He pays with a £5 note.

How much change does Max get?

8 How much does an apple cost?

 + + + = 95p

 + + = 75p

→ Practice book 4C p47

Unit 13
Time

In this unit we will ...

⚡ Convert between units of time
⚡ Write times in different ways
⚡ Compare times by converting units
⚡ Solve problems involving units of time

How many minutes are in 1 hour?

Here are some maths words we will be using. Are any of these words new?

convert   compare   units of time

seconds   minutes   hours

days   weeks   months

years   12-hour   24-hour

analogue   digital   am/pm

Which time do you think is shortest? Why?

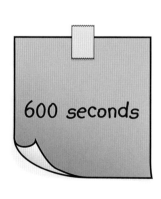

600 seconds

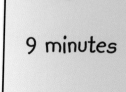

9 minutes

$\frac{1}{4}$ of an hour

Years, months, weeks and days

Discover

1 a) In how many days will the new play area open?

b) How old is Max's dog?

Share

a) The new play area will be open in 4 weeks. Convert this into days.

I drew a bar model to help me work out the number of days in 4 weeks.

4 weeks

I week	I week	I week	I week
7 days	7 days	7 days	7 days

28 days

I week = 7 days

4 × 7 = 28 days

The new play area will open in 28 days.

b) Max's dog is I year 7 months older than 3 years 8 months.

3 years + I year = 4 years

8 months + 7 months = 15 months

I added the number of whole years first. Then I added the number of months.

15 months	
12 months	3 months

I year   3 months

15 months is the same as I year and 3 months.

4 years + I year and 3 months = 5 years and 3 months

Max's dog is 5 years and 3 months old.

Think together

1

I am 8 years and 10 months old.

Reena

I am 4 months older than you.

Andy

a) How old is Andy?

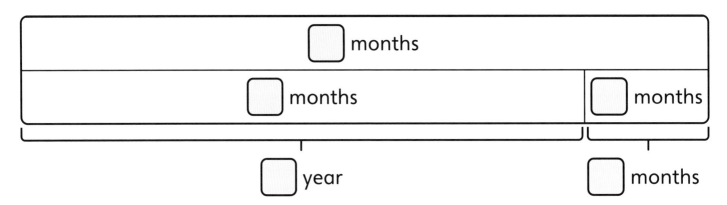

☐ months

☐ months   ☐ months

☐ year   ☐ months

b) Mo is 1 year and 11 months older than Reena.

How old is Mo?

2 How many weeks are the same as 35 days?

35 days
7 days

☐ × 7 days = ☐ weeks

35 ÷ 7 = ☐

☐ weeks are the same as 35 days.

3 What is 4 years and 3 months converted into months?

I think that 4 years and 3 months is the same as 43 months.

Amelia

I will think about how many months are in a year.

Explain Amelia's mistake.

Work out the correct answer.

71

→ Practice book 4C p49

Hours, minutes and seconds

Discover

1 **a)** How many seconds are there in 1 minute?

b) Do the two countdown timers show the same time until launch?

Share

a)

I minute
60 seconds

I minute is equal to 60 seconds.

b) The timers show the time in different ways.

200 seconds

3 minutes 20 seconds

To compare the times, convert them into the same **unit of time**.

I drew a bar model.

I minute = 60 seconds

3 minutes 20 seconds

I minute	I minute	I minute	20 seconds
60 seconds	60 seconds	60 seconds	20 seconds

3 × 60   20

200 seconds

3 minutes 20 seconds = 200 seconds

Both timers show the same time until launch.

I used the 6 times-table to help me multiply by 60.

73

Think together

1 Do these two timers show the same time? Use the bar model to help you.

2 minutes 50 seconds

1 minute	1 minute	50 seconds
60 seconds	60 seconds	50 seconds

2 × 60   50

☐ seconds

2 The countdown timer on the right is correct. The timer on the left is wrong.

What should the timer on the left show?

4 MINUTES 30 SECONDS

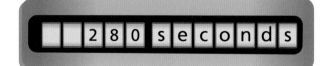

3 What is 5 hours and 10 minutes written in minutes?

Remember, there are 60 minutes in 1 hour.

5 hours and 10 minutes = ☐ minutes

How is this similar to converting minutes into seconds?

5 hours and 10 minutes

| 1 hour |
| 60 minutes |

☐ minutes ☐ seconds

I can see a pattern between converting minutes into seconds and converting hours into minutes.

75

Convert between analogue and digital times

Discover

I **a)** What should the time on the watch say now?

  b) Once the watch has been changed, what time will the clock and the watch show when the spies meet back at the bench?

Share

a) Analogue and digital are two ways of showing times. You can convert from one to the other.

The park clock shows an analogue time.

It shows the time is 7 minutes past 3.

The time on the watch should say 3:07 pm.

5 minutes
2 minutes

hour   minutes past

'am' times are before midday (starting from midnight); 'pm' times are after midday (up to midnight).

b) An hour and a half is the same as 1 hour 30 minutes.

3:07 pm   4:07 pm   4:37 pm

+ 1 hour   + 30 minutes

When the spies meet back at the bench, the clock and the watch will look like this:

analogue   digital

I knew that half an hour is 30 minutes because 1 hour is 60 minutes.

77

Think together

1 What will this time look like as an analogue time and as a digital time?

Twenty to 9 is the same as ☐ minutes past ☐.

2 Match the analogue and digital clocks.

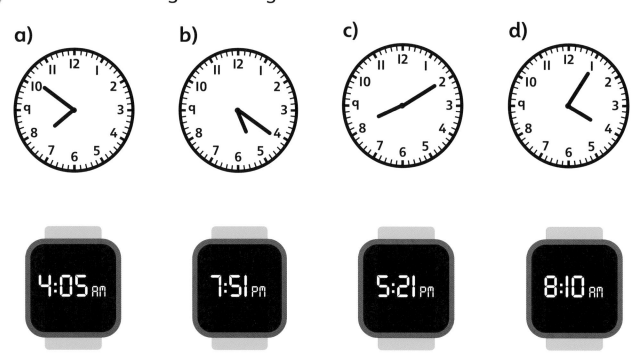

a)   b)   c)   d)

4:05 AM   7:51 PM   5:21 PM   8:10 AM

3 Jamilla, Alex and Bella have tried to draw this time on their clock faces.

Jamilla   Alex   Bella

a) Whose clock face matches the digital time?

b) What mistakes have the other two children made?

> I will look at the hour hand first, then the minute hand.

79

Convert to the 24-hour clock

Discover

All of these digital times have four digits.

Some of the times look unusual.

Richard

Luis

1 **a)** Why do the watches show four digits?

b) The analogue clock is correct. Which watch shows the right time?

Share

a) All the digital watches show **24-hour** times.

24-hour digital times are always written using four digits.

> 24-hour times do not include 'am' or 'pm'. We know by looking at the numbers. Times from 00:00 to 11:59 are am times. Times from 12:00 to 23:59 are pm times.

The first two digits show the hour (from 00 up to 23).

The last two digits show the number of minutes past (from 00 up to 59).

hours	:	minutes past
06	:	30
09	:	17
13	:	45
15	:	52
19	:	00

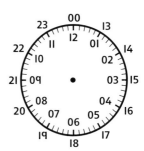

b) The time on the clock is 8 minutes to 4. This is the same as 52 minutes past 3.

The shop is open, so this is a pm time.

> I converted a **12-hour** pm time into a 24-hour time by adding 12 to the number of hours.

3 + 12 = 15

3:52 pm = 15:52

The correct watch looks like this:

81

Think together

 What will these times look like as 24-hour times?

a) The clock shows ☐ minutes past ☐.

As a 12-hour time, this is written as ☐ : ☐ am.

As a 24-hour time, this is written

as ☐ : ☐ .

in the
morning

b) The clock shows ☐ minutes to ☐.

As a 12-hour time, this is written as ☐ : ☐ pm.

☐ + 12 = ☐

As a 24-hour time, this is written as ☐ : ☐ .

at night

2 Quarter to 5 is the same as ☐ minutes past ☐.

How would you complete the analogue and 24-hour digital clock if this time was in the morning?

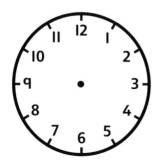   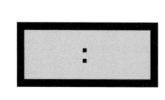

3 Mo is altering his digital watch to show 24-hour times.

It is twenty-five to 7.

a) What would Mo's watch show if this was an am time?

b) What would it show if it was a pm time?

4

I know how to convert this to a 24-hour time. I add 12 to the number of hours to get 19:28.

Isla

Explain Isla's mistake.

How would you convert 7:28 am into a 24-hour time?

I will think about how many digits a 24-hour time has.

83

Problem solving – convert units of time

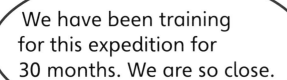

1. **a)** How many years have the explorers been training for this expedition?

   b) Does Toshi have enough socks to make it to the North Pole?

Share

I used a bar model to help me convert 30 months into years.

a) The explorers have been training for 30 months.

30 months		
12 months	12 months	6 months

1 year   1 year $\frac{1}{2}$ year

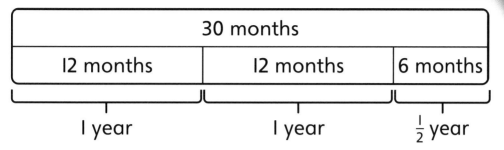

12 months = 1 year

6 months = $\frac{1}{2}$ a year

30 months = 12 months + 12 months + 6 months

The explorers have been training for $2\frac{1}{2}$ years.

b)

I converted the weeks into days to compare them.

3 weeks

I week	I week	I week
7 days	7 days	7 days

21 days

3 × 7 = 21

Toshi has enough socks for 21 days.

It takes 20 days to get to the North Pole. 21 days > 20 days.

Toshi does have enough socks to make it to the North Pole.

I found the same answer by converting the days into weeks instead. 3 weeks > 2 weeks 6 days.

Think together

1 Who is quicker at putting their socks on in the cold?

It takes me 3 minutes and 14 seconds to put my socks on in the cold.

Jen

It takes me 203 seconds.

Toshi

3 minutes 14 seconds

1 minute	1 minute	1 minute	14 seconds
☐ seconds	☐ seconds	☐ seconds	14 seconds

☐ seconds

_____ is quicker than _____ .

I can think of a different way to convert these times to find the answer.

2 Which tin of food needs to be used first?

Find the answer in two ways.

A   B

a) Convert tin A into weeks and compare the weeks.

Tin A

30 days

7 days	7 days	7 days	7 days	2 days
☐ week	☐ week	☐ week	☐ week	2 days

☐ weeks ☐ days

b) Convert tin B into days and compare the days.

3 How could you compare:

a) 3 hours and 45 minutes to 200 minutes?

b) $4\frac{1}{2}$ years to 50 months?

What operations did you use in each part?

To compare measurements, I will convert one of the measurements so that the units are the same in both.

87

→ Practice book 4C p61

End of unit check

1 It takes Alex 180 seconds to run around the school field.

What is another way of writing this time?

A 30 minutes

B 7,200 minutes

C 3 seconds

D 3 minutes

2 How could you find out the number of days in 21 weeks?

A Multiply 21 by 7.

B Divide 21 by 7.

C Change the units to 21 days.

D Subtract 7 from 21.

3 Which time is not the same as the others?

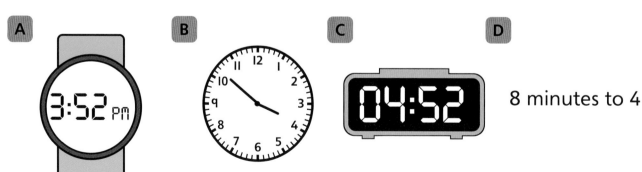

A   3:52 PM

B

C   04:52

D   8 minutes to 4

4 Which of these 12-hour times is written correctly as a 24-hour time?

A 2:34 am = 24:34

B 4:19 am = 04:19

C 7:30 am = 19:30

D 3:29 am = 3:29

5 Which of these lengths of time is the longest?

A 1 week   **B** 75 days   **C** 150 minutes   **D** 240 hours

6 Amelia, Bella and Ebo run a race.

Amelia's time is 85 seconds.

Bella finishes 8 seconds before Amelia.

I finished 2 seconds after Bella.

Ebo

What is Ebo's time in minutes and seconds?

→ **Practice book 4C p64**

Unit 14
Geometry – angles and 2D shapes

In this unit we will …

⚡ Learn to recognise obtuse, acute and right angles

⚡ Understand regular and irregular shapes

⚡ Name and describe quadrilaterals and triangles

⚡ Identify lines of symmetry in shapes and patterns

Do you remember quarter turns and half turns?

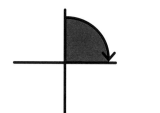

We will need some maths words.
Do you recognise any of these words?

quadrilateral   triangle   regular

irregular   interior angle   angle

acute   obtuse   polygon

right angle   symmetric

isosceles   scalene   equilateral

line of symmetry   reflective symmetry

Can you identify the right angle?
Describe it to a partner.

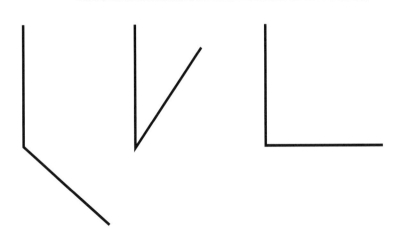

Identify angles

Discover

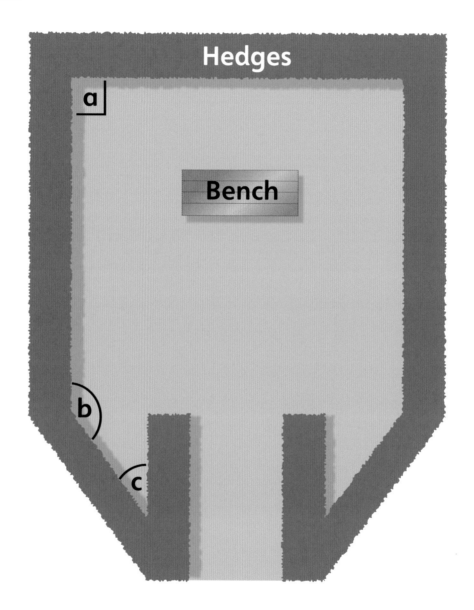

1. **a)** In which corners (**a**, **b** or **c**) of the garden can the bench be placed?

   b) Explain what is the same and what is different between angles **a**, **b** and **c**.

Share

a) Angle **a** is the same size as the angle of the corners of the bench, so it will fit neatly here.

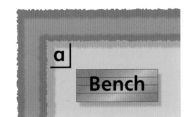

Angle **b** is larger than the angle of the corners of the bench, so it can be placed here.

Angle **c** is smaller than the angle of the corners of the bench, so it cannot be placed here.

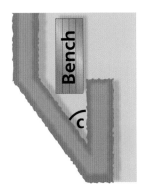

b) All of the angles measure the turn between two hedges of the garden.

Angle **a** is a quarter turn or a right angle.
Angle **b** is larger than a right angle.
Angle **c** is smaller than a right angle.

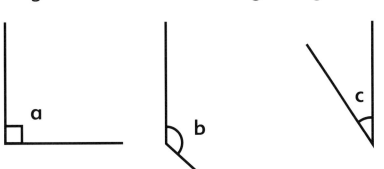

Acute is an angle less than a quarter turn. Obtuse is an angle greater than a quarter turn.

Think together

1 Which corners will the bench fit in?

Bench

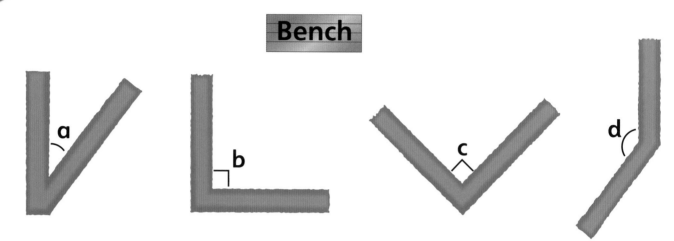

2 **a)** Which of these angles are acute?

b) Which of these angles are obtuse?

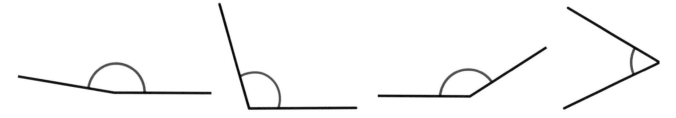

c) One of the angles in **a)** or **b)** is a right-angle. Which one?

Remember, acute is the name for an angle less than a right angle.

Obtuse is an angle greater than a right angle.

3 **a)** To which numbers could the clock hand point to show:

  i) an acute turn

  ii) a right-angle turn

  iii) an obtuse turn

b) Here is a kite.

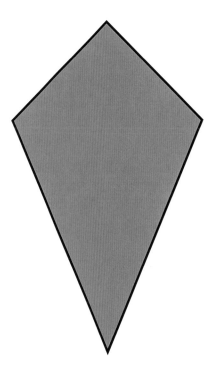

Describe the angles in the kite.

95

Compare and order angles

Discover

Emma

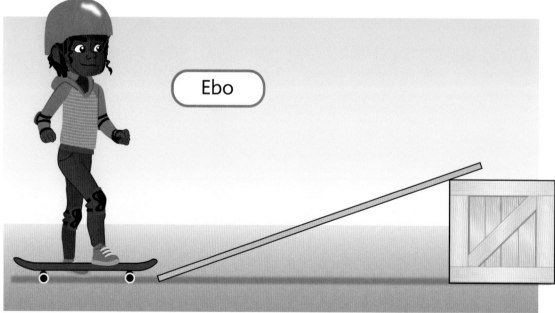

Ebo

1 **a)** Which ramp will allow the highest jump?

b) At what angle would each ramp stop working as a ramp?

Share

a) The children have set their ramps up at different angles. Emma's ramp has a greater angle than Ebo's ramp.

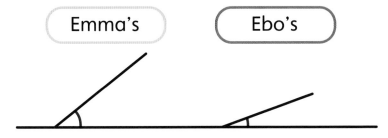

As Emma's ramp is set to a greater angle than Ebo's, she would be able to jump the highest from her ramp.

> Both of these angles are smaller than a right angle. Remember, an angle less than a right angle is called an acute angle.

b) A ramp set at a right angle would not work as a ramp.

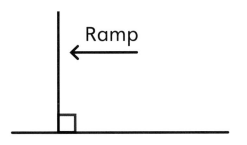

If the angle increases past a right angle, the ramps will work as ramps from the other direction.

> I think that some acute angles will also not work.

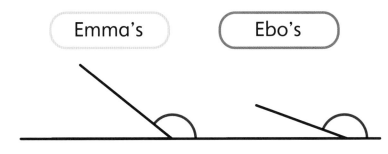

Think together

1 a) Point to the smallest angle.

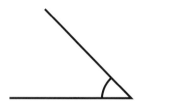 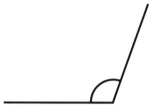

b) Point to the largest angle.

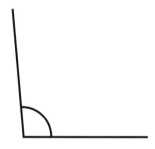 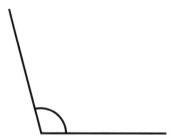

c) Point to the smallest angle.

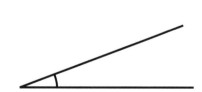 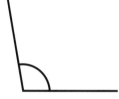

2 Put the following angles in order of smallest to greatest.

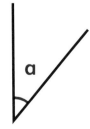 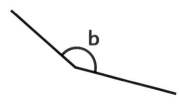 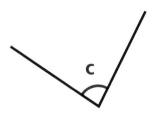 

3

A

B

C

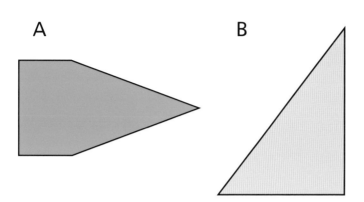

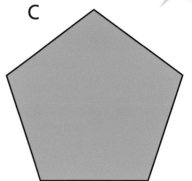

a) Order the three shapes. Complete the table by filling in all three columns for each category. One has been done for you.

Fewest acute angles		Most acute angles
Fewest right angles		Most right angles
C		
Fewest obtuse angles		Most obtuse angles

b) Order the angles in the triangle from greatest to smallest.

99

Triangles

Discover

Ambika

Lee

1 **a)** Ambika folds a square piece of paper in half diagonally.
Lee folds a rectangular piece of paper in half diagonally.
What shapes have they made?

b) How are their triangles similar and how are they different?

Share

a) When folded in half, both the square and the rectangular pieces of paper create types of triangles.

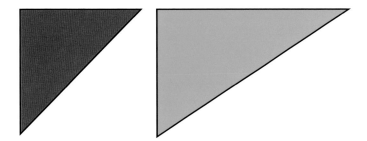

Ambika and Lee have made triangles.

b) Both triangles have a right angle.

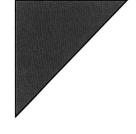

The square makes a triangle that has two equal sides and two equal angles. This is called an **isosceles** triangle.

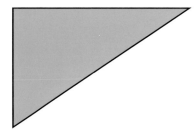

The rectangle makes a triangle that has three unequal sides and three unequal angles. This is called a **scalene** triangle.

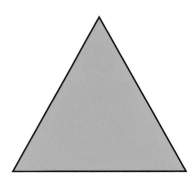

This is another type of triangle. A triangle that has three equal sides and three equal angles is called an **equilateral** triangle.

Think together

1 Which of these triangles is a scalene triangle?

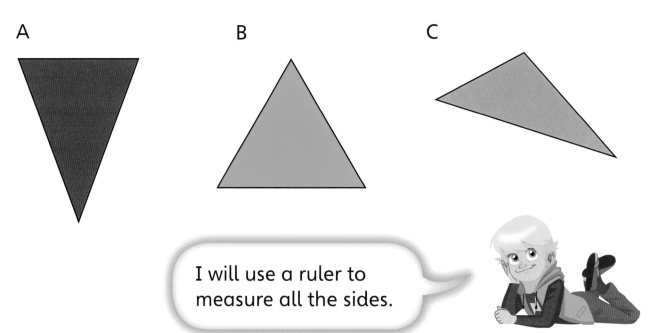

A   B   C

I will use a ruler to measure all the sides.

2 Which of these isosceles triangles have three acute angles?

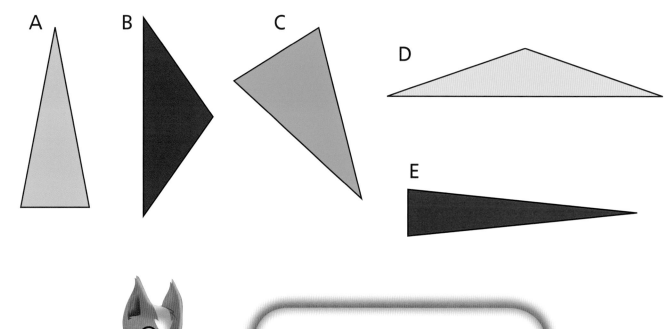

A   B   C   D   E

Remember, an acute angle is less than a quarter turn.

3 **a)** How many different triangles can you make on a 3×3 geoboard?

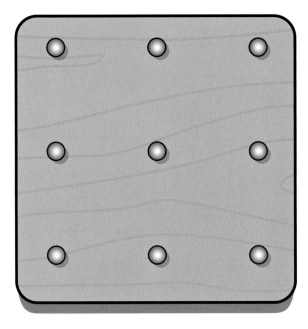

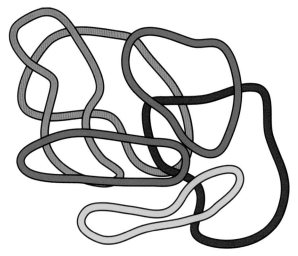

b) Have you found them all? How do you know?

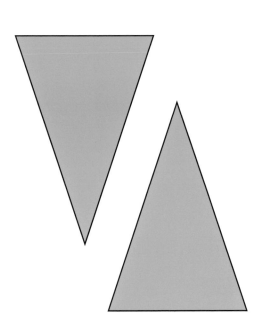

> I wonder whether these triangles are different. Perhaps they are the same but rotated.

103

Quadrilaterals

Discover

Olivia

1 **a)** Olivia is making shapes with geostrips. What is the same and what is different about the shapes she has made?

b) Which shape is a regular quadrilateral?

Share

a) Quadrilaterals can have different lengths and different angles from each other.

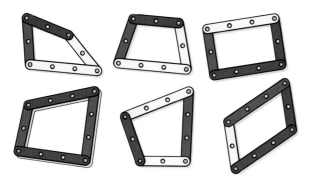

> I remembered that a polygon with four sides is called a quadrilateral.

Olivia's shapes all have four sides but each has different angles.

b) A quadrilateral with four equal sides is called a rhombus. The **interior angles** of a rhombus may be different but its sides are all the same length.

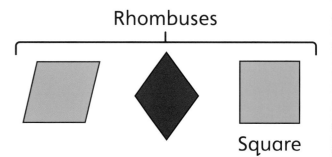

Rhombuses

Square

A square is the only regular quadrilateral and is a special type of rhombus. It has four equal sides and four equal angles.

> I remembered that only one thing needs to be different for a shape to be irregular.

Regular	Irregular
All sides are equal. All interior angles are equal.	Interior angles and/or sides are unequal.

Think together

1 A parallelogram is a quadrilateral that has two pairs of parallel sides. Identify all the parallelograms.

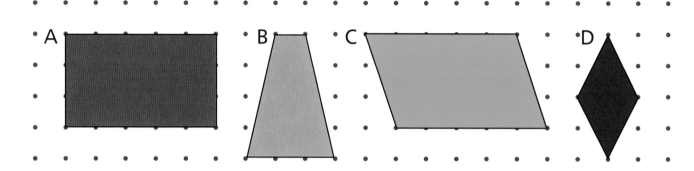

How do you know?

> Remember, parallel lines are two lines that are always the same distance apart and never touch.

2 A trapezium has one pair of parallel sides. The other pair of sides can be the same length or different lengths.

Draw a different trapezium to the one pictured here. Use squared paper to help you.

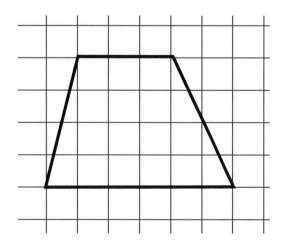

> I wonder if a parallelogram is a kind of trapezium.

3 **a)** What quadrilaterals can you create by drawing lines between the points like those below?

b) Organise your shapes into sorting circles like this.

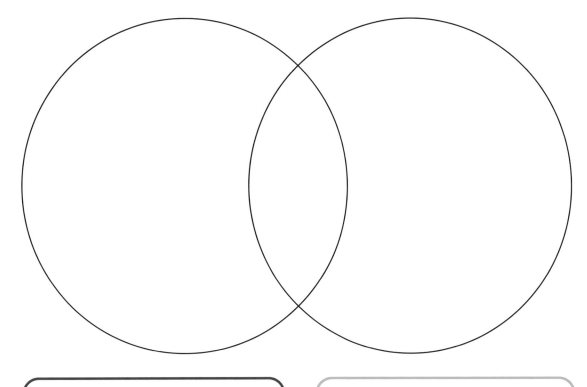

Contains a right angle   Sides the same length

→ **Practice book 4C p75**

Polygons

Discover

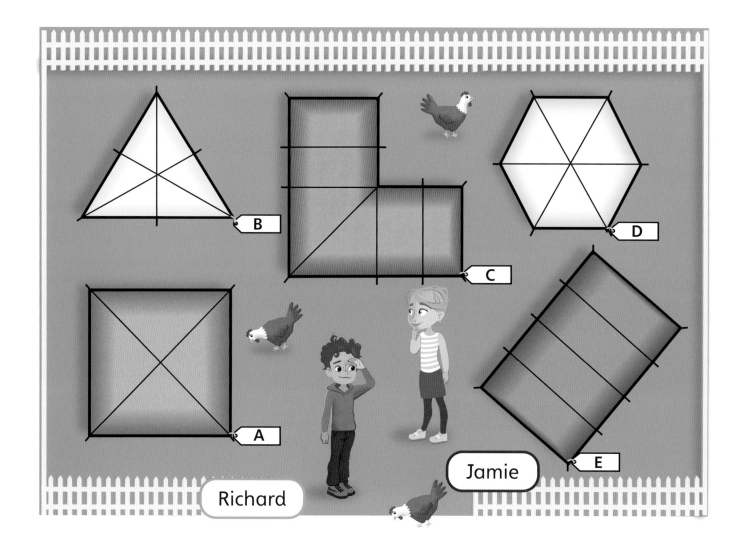

1 a) Richard remembers losing his favourite toy car near a hexagonal tent. Which tent could it have been?

b) Explain how the two hexagons are both similar and different.

Share

a) All hexagons have six sides and six vertices. There are two hexagonal tent outlines on the campsite.

Richard's toy car could be near either tent C or D.

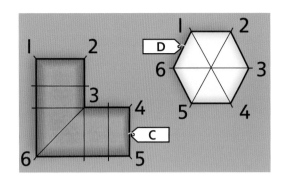

b)

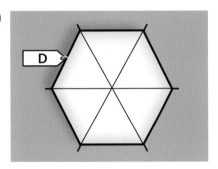

This hexagon has six sides that are all equal. It also has six interior angles that are all equal. This means it is a regular hexagon.

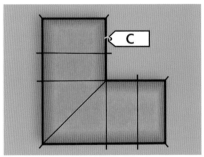

This hexagon also has six sides but they are different lengths. It also has six interior angles but they are also different sizes. This means it is an irregular hexagon.

I knew that interior angles are the angles inside a polygon.

A shape is regular only if all sides are the same length **and** all angles are the same size.

The two hexagons are similar because they both have six sides and six angles. They are different because their side lengths and interior angles are different sizes.

Think together

1 Which of these polygons are irregular?

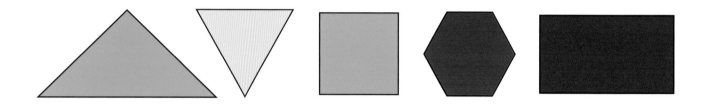

2 Which polygons in this picture are regular and which are irregular? How do you know?

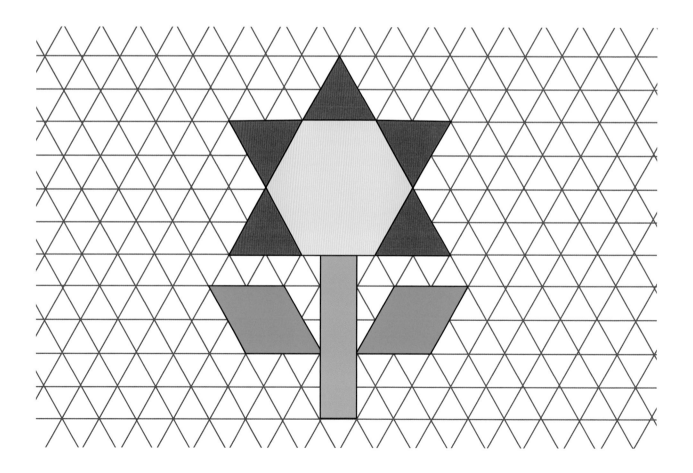

3 Alex has sorted some shapes. Has she sorted them correctly?

	Irregular	Regular
A 4-sided polygon	parallelogram	rectangle
Not a 4-sided polygon	hexagon	equilateral triangle and isosceles triangle

Name another polygon that could go in each section.

III

Reason about polygons

Discover

1 **a)** Bella has made a polygon by overlapping two pieces of square paper. Explain why Bella's polygon cannot be a regular hexagon.

What other polygons could Bella make?

b) What polygon could Bella make with the largest number of vertices?

Share

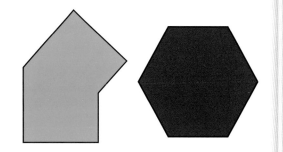

a) The polygon Bella has made cannot be a regular hexagon because the sides are not equal and the angles are not equal.

Regular polygons have equal length sides and equal angles.

Bella could use her squares of paper to create shapes such as these.

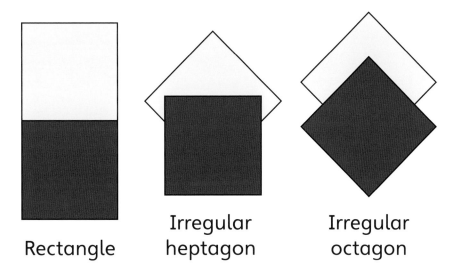

Rectangle

Irregular heptagon

Irregular octagon

b) To make the polygon with the largest number of vertices, Bella should arrange the two squares like this:

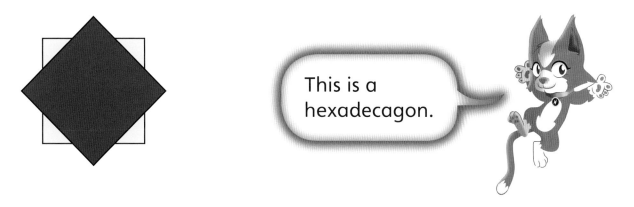

This is a hexadecagon.

Think together

1 Raj makes this shape with two different quadrilateral pieces of paper.

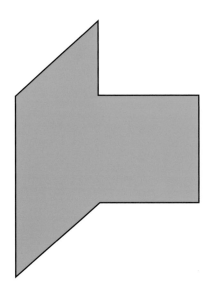

What shapes could the pieces of paper have been?

2 Ruby has five equilateral triangles. She joins them along their edges to make different shapes.

Ruby has made a rhombus using two of the triangles.

What different shapes can she make?
(She does not have to use them all.)

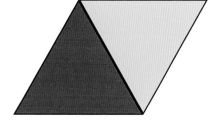

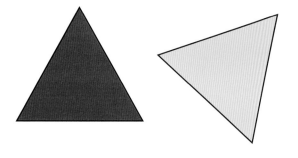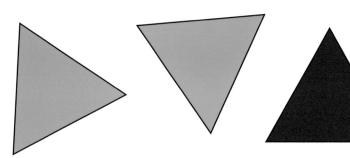

Prove your ideas.

3 **a)** Jamilla has made a pentagon by shading the area where two square pieces of paper overlap. What other shapes could Jamilla make in this way?

Jamilla

b) Can she make all the different types of quadrilateral?

Use the table to help you.

Quadrilateral	Can it be made?
Square	
Rectangle	
Rhombus	
Trapezium	
Kite	
Arrowhead	

I wonder if Jamilla can make a regular pentagon.

115

Lines of symmetry

Discover

1 **a)** How many lines of symmetry can you find for a square?

b) How many lines of symmetry are there in an equilateral triangle?

Share

a)

I cut out a square and folded it in different ways.

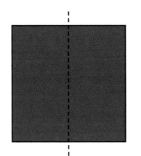 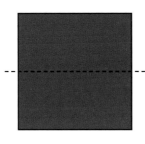 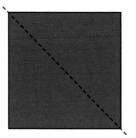 

There are four lines of symmetry inside a square.

b)

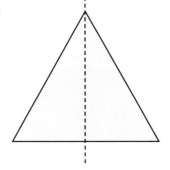 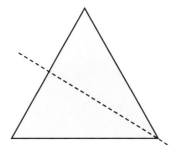 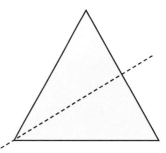

In an equilateral triangle, there are three lines of symmetry.

An equilateral triangle has three lines of **reflective symmetry**. This means a mirror held on that line will show the whole shape exactly.

Think together

1   Dominic says, 'This is a line of symmetry in this rectangle.'
Is he correct? Explain your reasoning.

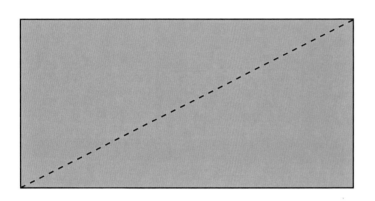

I will try folding a rectangular piece of paper to check.

2   How many lines of symmetry do these two hexagons have?

A

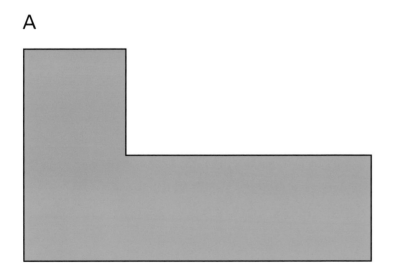

B

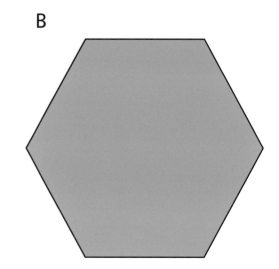

3 Identify the lines of symmetry in these polygons.

CHALLENGE

I will use a mirror to check.

I think some of these shapes do not have any lines of symmetry.

→ Practice book 4C p84

Complete a symmetric figure

Isla

1 Isla is building a symmetric, octagonal pen for her chickens.
She has used five pieces of fence so far.

a) She uses five more lengths of fence.

What does her chicken pen look like?

How many lines of symmetry does it have?

b) Could she complete a symmetric pattern with fewer than
five more pieces of fence?

Share

a) Isla's chicken pen will look like this once it has been completed with five more pieces of fence.

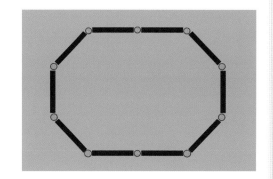

This shape has two lines of symmetry.

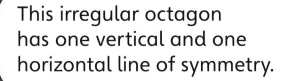

This irregular octagon has one vertical and one horizontal line of symmetry.

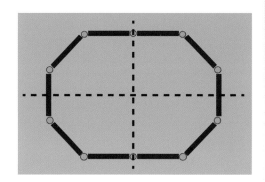

b) Isla could complete a symmetric, octagonal pen by using only three more pieces of fence. This is what the pen would look like.

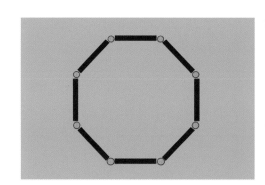

This regular octagon has 8 lines of symmetry.

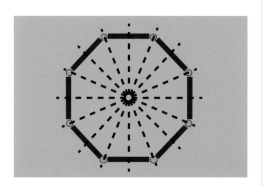

Think together

1 Complete the symmetric figures using lolly sticks.

a)

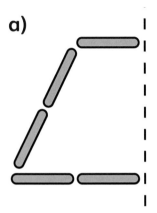

b)

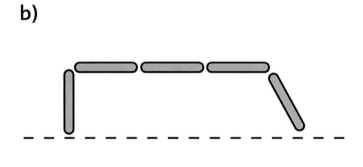

2 Complete these symmetric shapes made of lolly sticks.

a)

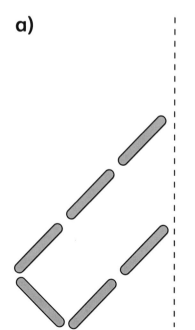

b)

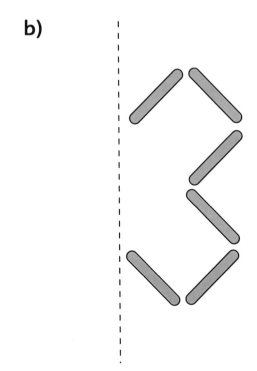

3 Kate thinks three things about symmetric shapes.

Prove which are true and which are false.

Use squared paper to help you.

I can draw a quadrilateral that makes a pentagon when I reflect it along one side.

If half my shape has three sides then the reflected shape must be a hexagon.

If I reflect a shape the number of sides always doubles.

Kate

123

End of unit check

1 Identify the irregular quadrilateral.

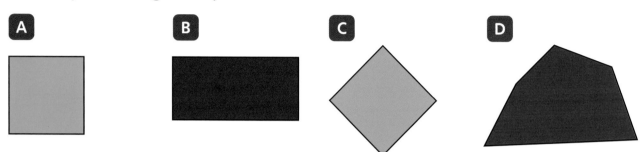

2 Which angle is obtuse?

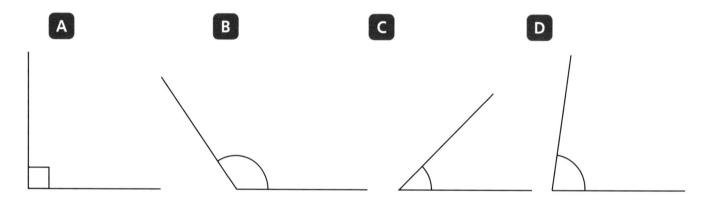

3 Identify the isosceles triangle.

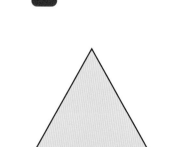

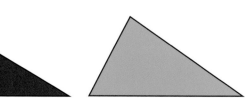

4 Identify the shape that has more than three obtuse angles.

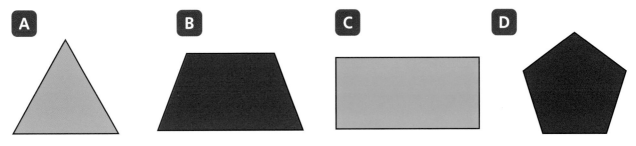

A   B   C   D

5 Identify the shape with two lines of symmetry.

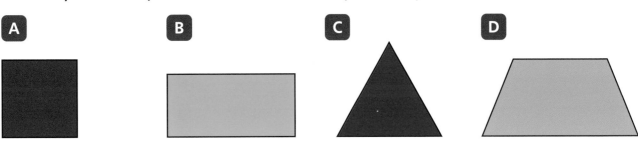

A   B   C   D

6 This square has been divided into four triangles **A**, **B**, **C** and **D**.

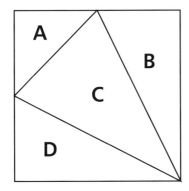

a) Which triangles have a **right angle**?

b) Which triangles have **two equal sides**?

125

→ Practice book 4C p90

Unit 15
Statistics

In this unit we will ...

⚡ Present data in pictograms, bar charts and tables

⚡ Solve problems based on data

⚡ Explore line graphs

We are going to meet this type of graph in this unit. What was the temperature at 10 am?

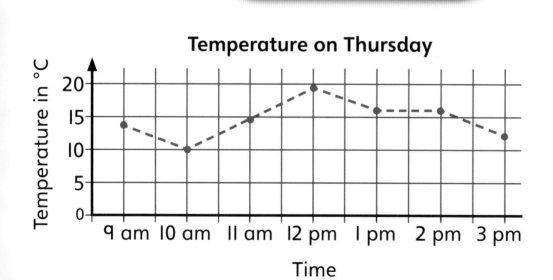

Temperature on Thursday

We will need some maths words. Which ones have you seen before?

data | line graph | pictogram
bar chart | table | altogether
more than | compare

We need this too! How many people's favourite colour is yellow?

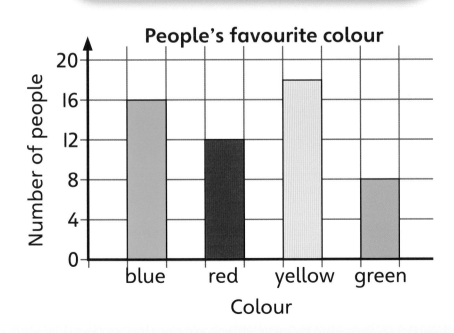

People's favourite colour

Number of people vs Colour (blue, red, yellow, green)

Interpret charts

Discover

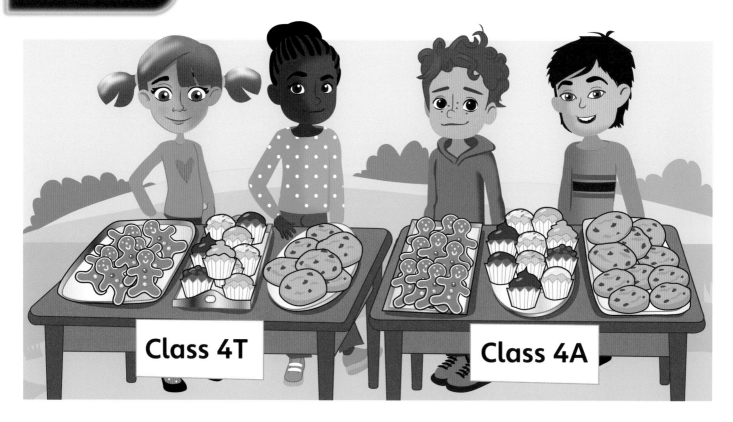

Number of items baked by Class 4T

	Number
cupcakes	◯ ◯ ◯ ◯ ◯
gingerbread biscuits	◯ ◯ ◯ ◯
cookies	◯ ◯ ◯ ◯ ◖

Each ◯ represents 10 items.

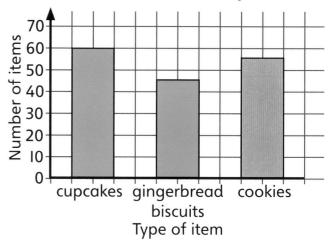

Number of items baked by Class 4A

① **a)** How many cookies did each class make?

b) Which item did Class 4A make the most of? How many did they make?

128

Share

a) Each ◯ in the pictogram represents 10 items.

Each ◖ represents 5 items.

The row for cookies has 4 and a half ◯.

◯ ◯ ◯ ◯ ◖
10 + 10 + 10 + 10 + 5 = 45

Class 4T made 45 cookies.

> I did it another way. I multiplied 4 × 10 then added 5.

In the bar chart, the bar for cookies lines up half-way between 50 and 60 on the vertical axis.

Class 4A made 55 cookies.

> I used a ruler to make sure I read the correct values.

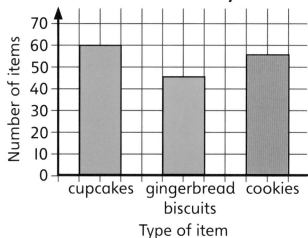

Number of items baked by Class 4A

b) The highest bar in the bar chart is for cupcakes.

Class 4A made more cupcakes than any other item.

The top of the cupcake bar lines up with 60 on the vertical axis.

Class 4A made 60 cupcakes.

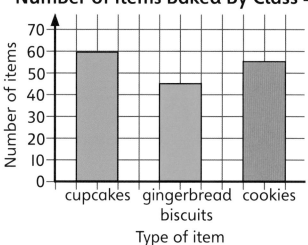

Number of items baked by Class 4A

Think together

The charts show the number of items sold by Class 5T and Class 5A.

Number of items sold by Class 5T

	Number
cupcakes	○ ○ ○ ◖
gingerbread biscuits	○ ○ ○ ◔
cookies	○ ○ ○ ○ ○

Each ○ represents 8 items.

Number of items sold by Class 5A

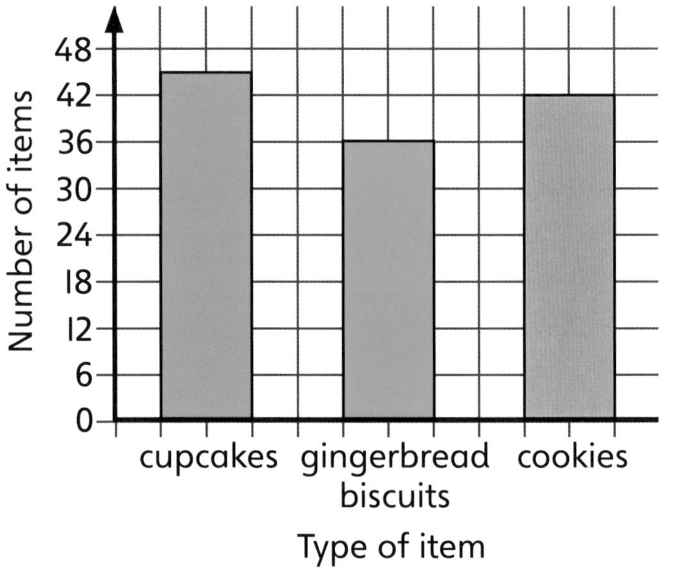

1 **a)** How many cupcakes did each class sell?

b) How many gingerbread biscuits did Class 5T sell?

I think ◔ must represent a quarter of a ○.

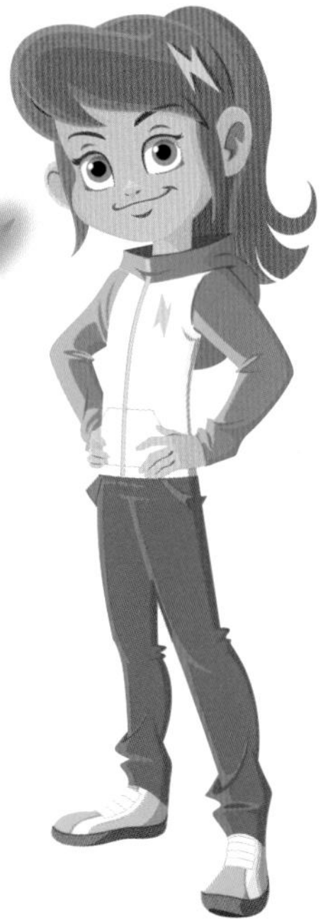

2 The table shows how many cupcakes and gingerbread biscuits two more classes sold.

	Class 4B	Class 4C
Cupcakes	8	15
Gingerbread biscuits	12	6

Cupcakes were sold for £2. Gingerbread biscuits were sold for £1.

Which class raised the most money?

3 Some children are raising money for charity. The bar chart shows the amount each year group raised.

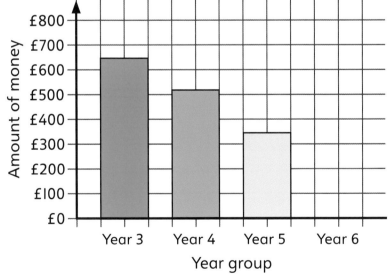

a) How much did Year 3 raise?

b) Year 6 raised £675.

The bar for Year 6 should be half-way between £600 and £700.

Olivia

Is Olivia correct?

Explain your answer.

c) How much did the year groups raise altogether?

131

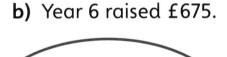

→ **Practice book 4C p93**

Solve problems with charts ❶

Discover

Number of tickets sold on Saturday

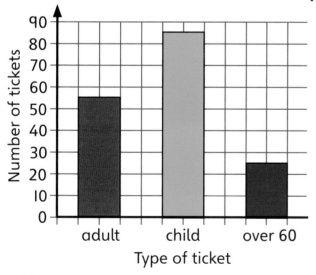

Number of tickets (y-axis)
Type of ticket (x-axis): adult, child, over 60

Number of tickets sold on Sunday

	Number of tickets
adult	▢ ▢ ▢ ▢ ◖
child	▢ ▢ ▢ ▢ ▢ ◖
over 60	▢ ▢ ◖

Each ▢ represents 12 tickets.

❶ **a)** How many more child tickets did the farm park sell on Saturday compared to Sunday?

b) How many adult (under 60) tickets did the farm park sell altogether over the weekend?

132

Share

a) The bar for child tickets is half-way between 80 and 90.

85 child tickets were sold on Saturday.

5 × 12 = 60
60 + 6 = 66

The farm park sold 66 child tickets on Sunday.

85 − 66 = 19

The farm park sold 19 more child tickets on Saturday.

Number of tickets sold on Saturday

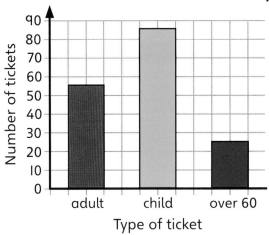

Type of ticket

Number of tickets sold on Sunday

child	□ □ □ □ □ ⊏

Each □ represents 12 people.
Each ⊏ represents 6 people.

b) The farm park sold 55 adult tickets on Saturday.

There are four and a half symbols for adult tickets on the pictogram.

4 × 12 = 48
48 + 6 = 54

The farm park sold 54 adult tickets on Sunday.

55 + 54 = 109

The farm park sold 109 adult tickets altogether over the weekend.

> I added a value from the bar chart to a value on the pictogram.

133

Think together

① The charts show the number of children and adults feeding baby animals.

Number of children feeding baby animals

	Number of children
lambs	
calves	
foals	

Each ⬤ represents 12 children.

Number of adults feeding baby animals

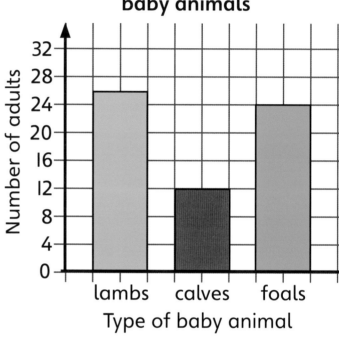

a) How many more children than adults fed the lambs?

b) How many people fed the foals altogether?

I will work out first how many children fed the animals.

2 The pictograms show the amount of money made at a café on Saturday and Sunday.

Money made from meals sold on Saturday

	Money
adult hot	◯◯◖
adult cold	◯◕
child hot	◯◯◹
child cold	◯◯◯

Each ◯ represents £100.

Money made from meals sold on Sunday

	Money
adult hot	◯◯◹
adult cold	◯◖
child hot	◯◯◯◕
child cold	◯◯◹

Each ◯ represents £100.

a) How much money did the café make from hot meals on Sunday?

b) How much more money did the café make from cold children's meals on Saturday compared to Sunday?

3 The bar chart shows the opinion of visitors to a farm on Saturday and Sunday.

a) How many more visitors rated the farm ok on Saturday than Sunday?

b) Did more people give the farm a rating on Saturday or Sunday?

■ represents Saturday

☐ represents Sunday

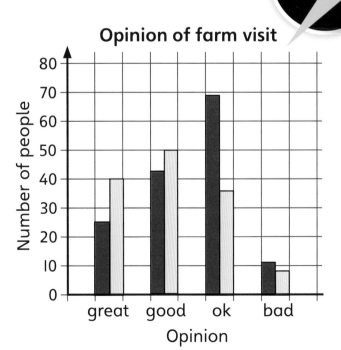

Opinion of farm visit

135

Solve problems with charts ❷

Discover

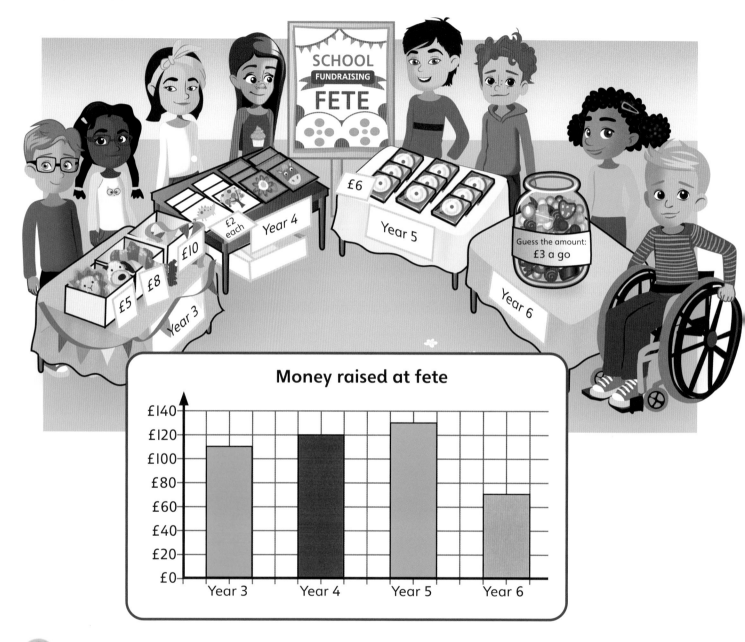

Money raised at fete

1 **a)** How much more money did Years 3 and 4 raise in total compared to Years 5 and 6?

b) Year 4 raised money by selling cards for £2 each.

How many cards did they sell in total?

Share

First, I worked out how much Years 3 and 4 raised altogether.

a) Year 3 raised £110.

Year 4 raised £120.

£120 + £110 = £230

Years 3 and 4 raised £230 altogether.

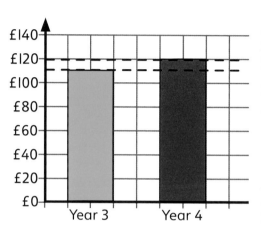

Year 5 raised £130.

Year 6 raised £70.

£130 + £70 = £200

Years 5 and 6 raised £200 altogether.

£230 − £200 = £30

Years 3 and 4 raised £30 more than Years 5 and 6.

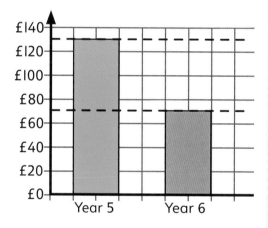

b) Year 4 raised £120.

£120 ÷ £2 = 60

Year 4 sold 60 cards in total.

I divided to work out how many cards Year 4 sold.

Think together

1. This bar chart shows how much money was raised by different classes.

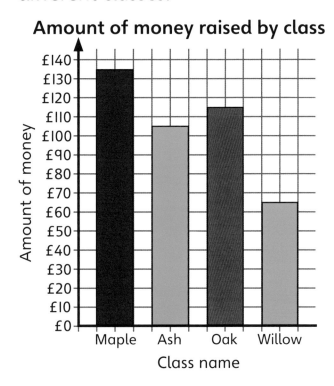

Amount of money raised by class

a) How much more money did Maple and Ash classes raise in total compared to Oak and Willow classes?

b) How much money did the four classes raise altogether?

c) Each child in Oak class raised £5.
   How many children are in Oak class?

I can use some of my working from part a) to help me work out part b).

2 The pictogram shows the number of soft toys Year 3 sold at a summer fair.

Type of soft toy sold by Year 3

a) Which soft toys did Year 3 sell more than 10 of?

b) Each soft toy sold for £5.

How much money was made by selling lions and dogs?

	Number
lions	⬤⬤⬤⬤⬤⬤⬤
dogs	⬤⬤⬤
cats	⬤◖
owls	⬤⬤⬤⬤⬤◖

Each ⬤ represents 2 soft toys.

3 Year 5 raised money by selling recordings of a class concert. Oak class sold 7 recordings. Each class sold recordings for the same amount.

Use the clues below to complete the table and work out how much money they raised in total.

Maple	£ ⬜
Ash	£ ⬜
Oak	£42
Willow	£ ⬜

I am going to work out how much Oak charged for each recording first.

Willow collected £12 less than Oak.

Maple collected $\frac{8}{10}$ of the amount Willow collected.

Ash collected $\frac{1}{2}$ more than Maple's total amount.

139

Interpret line graphs ❶

Discover

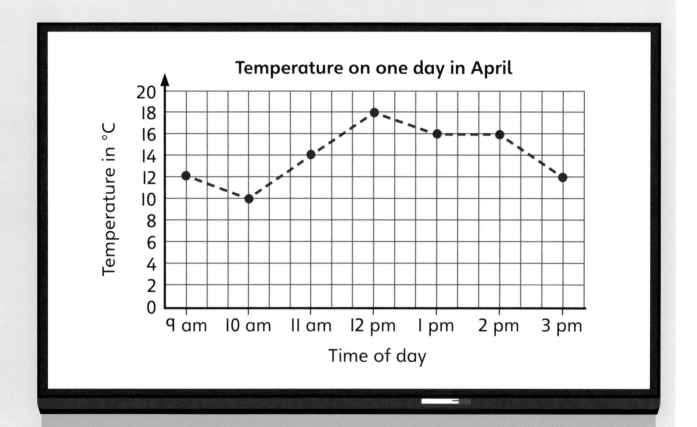

WEATHER STATION

Temperature on one day in April

❶ **a)** What was the temperature at 11 am?

b) How much did the temperature decrease by between 12 pm and 3 pm?

Share

a) Find 11 am on the horizontal axis of the line graph.

Then move up to meet the line.

Read along to see which temperature this corresponds to.

The temperature at 11 am is 14 °C.

> I used a ruler to help me.

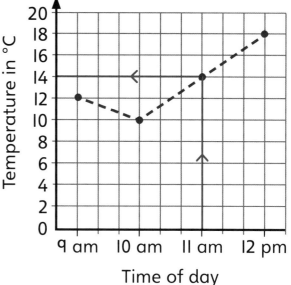

b) The temperature at 12 pm is 18 °C.

The temperature at 3 pm is 12 °C.

18 − 12 = 6

The temperature decreases by 6 °C between 12 pm and 3 pm.

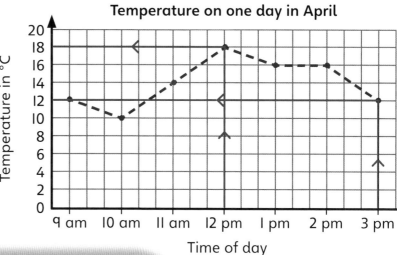

Temperature on one day in April

> I read off the values from 12 pm and 3 pm and found the difference.

Think together

This line graph shows the temperature inside Emily's house on Tuesday.

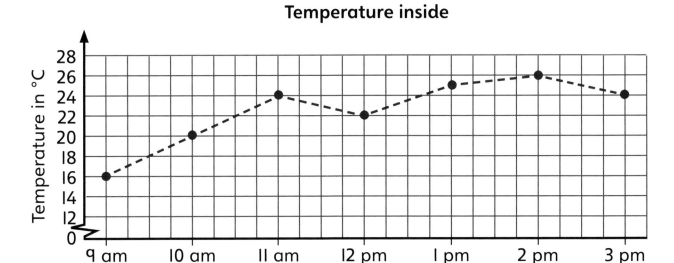

Temperature inside

① a) What was the temperature at 11 am?

b) What was the temperature at 1 pm?

c) Estimate the temperature at 2:30 pm. Explain why it is only an estimate.

d) At what time was it the warmest inside Emily's house?

e) At what time was the temperature 21 °C?

② For how long is the temperature above 24 °C in Emily's house?

I am going to start by going across from the temperature on the vertical axis.

3 The temperature in a small town was measured on 1 October and 1 December.

The results are shown on the line graph below.

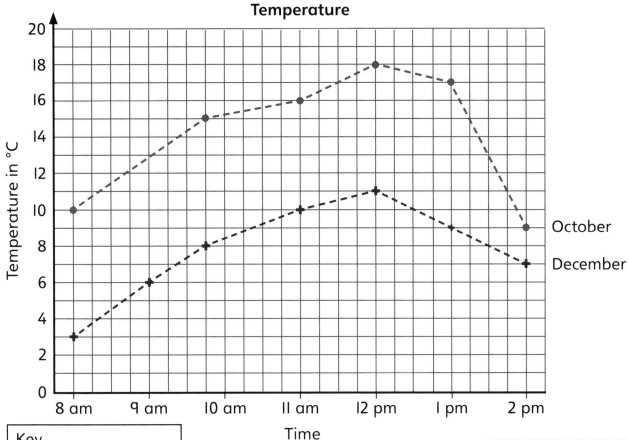

Key
October – – – – – –
December – – – – – –

a) What was the temperature at midday on 1 December?

b) What is the difference in the temperature at 2 pm on 1 December and 2 pm on 1 October?

c) What is the same and what is different about the temperatures on 1 October and 1 December?

Line graphs can show more than one set of data. Each set of data has its own line.

143

→ Practice book 4C p102

Interpret line graphs ②

Discover

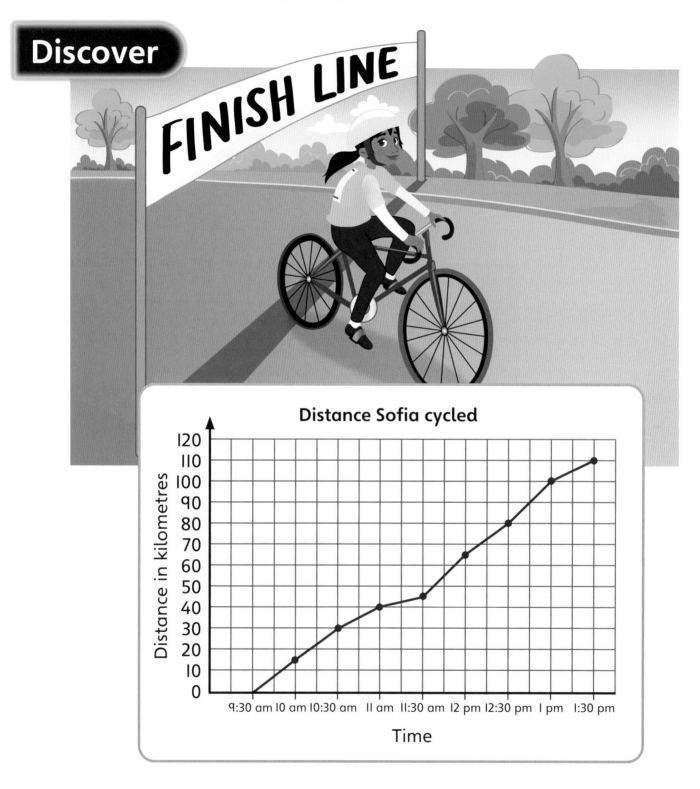

Distance Sofia cycled

1 **a)** How far did Sofia cycle between 11 am and 12 pm?

b) How long did it take Sofia to cycle the next 40 km after 12 pm?

Share

> I worked out the distance Sofia had cycled at 11 am and at 12 pm and then found the difference.

a) At 11 am, Sofia had cycled 40 km.

At 12 pm, Sofia had cycled 65 km.

65 − 40 = 25

Sofia cycled 25 km between 11 am and 12 pm.

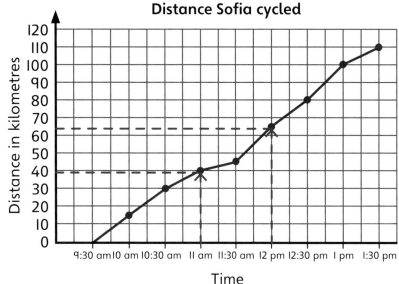

Distance Sofia cycled

b) Sofia had cycled 65 km by 12 pm.

65 + 40 = 105 km

Sofia had cycled 105 km by 1:15 pm.

It took Sofia 1 hour and 15 minutes to cycle the next 40 km.

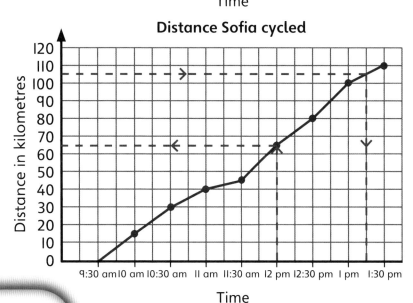

Distance Sofia cycled

> The data is **continuous**, so any point on the graph shows how far Sofia has cycled.

> I started by working out how many miles Sofia had travelled at 12 pm.

Think together

1 Toshi takes part in a cycle race. The line graph shows Toshi's journey.

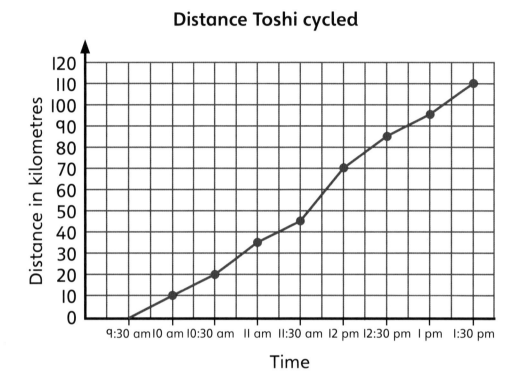

Distance Toshi cycled

a) How far did Toshi cycle between 12:30 pm and 1:30 pm?

b) How far did Toshi cycle between 11:15 am and 12:45 pm?

c) What time do you think the race started?

d) Do you think it is the same race that Sofia took part in?

2 How long did it take Toshi to cycle from 20 km to 70 km?

I will start by finding the time when Toshi had cycled 20 km.

CHALLENGE

3 This line graph shows the progress of two athletes in a running race.

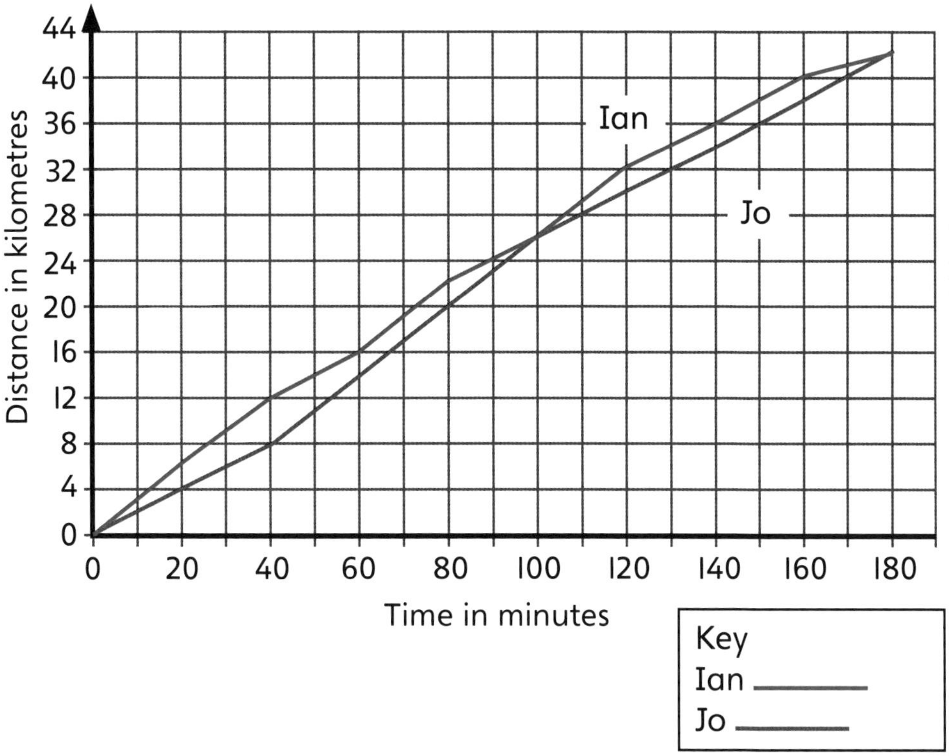

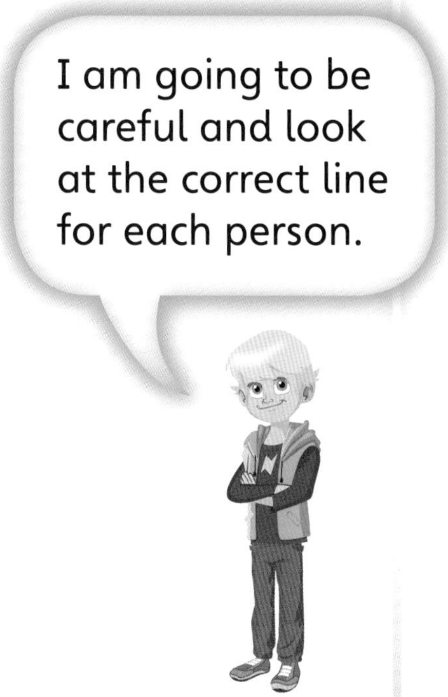

Distance in kilometres
0
4
8
12
16
20
24
28
32
36
40
44
Time in minutes
0
20
40
60
80
100
120
140
160
180
Ian
Jo
Key
Ian
Jo

I am going to be careful and look at the correct line for each person.

a) Complete these sentences.

After 60 minutes, Ian had run [ ] km and Jo had run [ ] km.

It took Jo [ ] minutes and Ian [ ] minutes to run 34 km.

Before the end of a race, Ian and Jo had both run exactly the same distance after [ ] minutes.

The length of the running race was [ ] km.

b) Write five more things that you can tell from the line graph.

Use some of the words below to help you.

most, compared to, least, fastest, slowest, further, more, less

→ Practice book 4C p105

Draw line graphs

Discover

Population of Blockley

Year	Population
1930	1,500
1940	1,800
1950	2,000
1960	2,500
1970	3,200
1980	4,000
1990	4,400
2000	4,500
2010	4,700
2020	4,800

Emma

1 **a)** Emma wants to draw a line graph to show how the population of her village has increased. What will each axis show?

b) Draw a line graph to represent this data.

Share

a) Time always goes on the horizontal axis. It will go from 1930 to 2020. The population will go on the vertical axis.

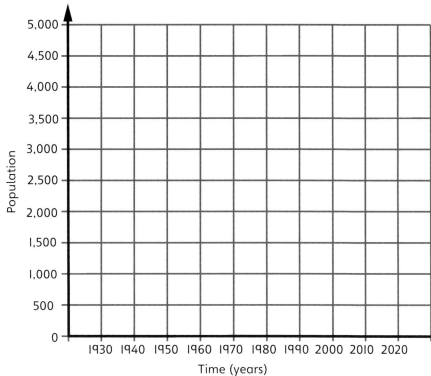

b)

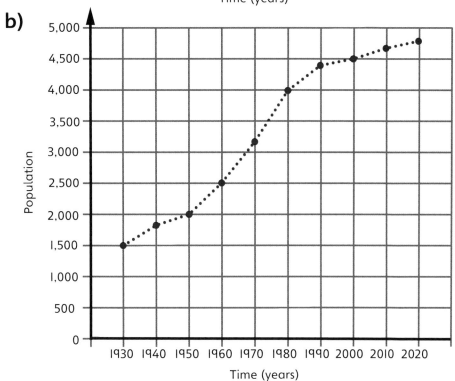

I used a dotted line as I didn't know the values between the years. The dotted lines helped me see the trend.

Think together

1 Aki is running a race. The table shows his progress.

	Distance from start	Time at checkpoint
Checkpoint A	5 km	25 minutes
Checkpoint B	8 km	60 minutes
Checkpoint C	10 km	80 minutes
Finish	12 km	95 minutes

Draw a line graph to represent this information.

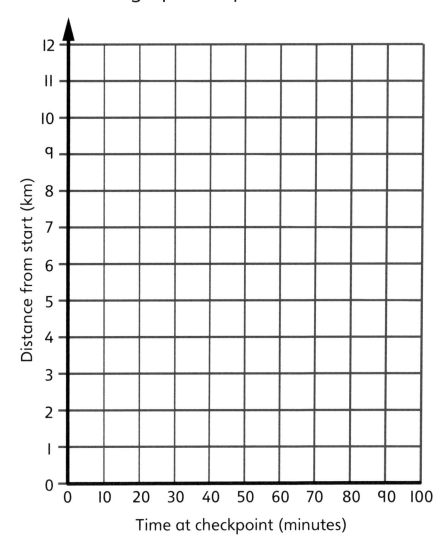

2 Use the line graph you have drawn from question I to answer these questions.

    a) Estimate how far Aki has run after 30 minutes.

    b) Estimate how long it took Aki to run 6 km.

    c) Why are your answers only estimates?

3 Conduct an experiment as a class. You will need:
  • an empty yoghurt pot with a small hole in the bottom
  • water
  • a measuring jug
  • a timer.

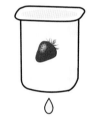

CHALLENGE

Hold the yoghurt pot over the measuring jug and pour water into the yoghurt pot. Measure the volume of water every I minute for 10 minutes.

Make a line graph of your results.

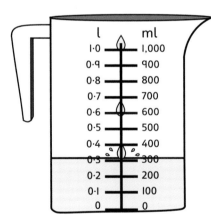

I wonder if the jug will fill at a steady speed.

I will predict the volume after each minute.

151

→ Practice book 4C p108

End of unit check

1 This pictogram shows people's favourite pet.
How many more people prefer a cat than prefer a rabbit?

A $1\frac{3}{4}$

C 9

B 7

D 10

People's favourite pet

	Number of people
cat	◯◯◯◯◁
dog	◯◯◯
rabbit	◯◯◖
hamster	◯◯◯◖

Each ◯ represents 4 people.

2 Use the pictogram in Question 1 to work out which of these statements is not true.

A The most popular pet is a cat.

B The least popular pet is a rabbit.

C 4 more people like hamsters than like rabbits.

D 3 people's favourite pet is a dog.

3 This table shows the scores out of 100 of 4 children in their termly spelling tests.

Which child showed the biggest improvement between Autumn term and Summer term?

A Otis

C Evie

B Grace

D Milo

	Autumn term	Summer term
Otis	73	93
Grace	21	71
Evie	42	93
Milo	32	81

4 Sam asked some children in Year 4 how they travelled to school.

He put his results in a bar chart.

How many children came by scooter?

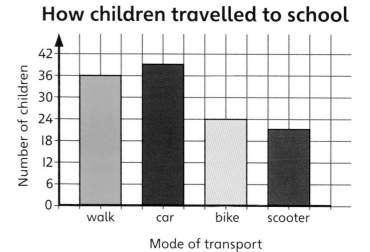

How children travelled to school

Number of children / Mode of transport

A 20

C 21

B 24

D 18 $\frac{1}{2}$

5 Use the bar model in Question 4 to work out how many more children walked, biked or used a scooter to get to school in total, compared to the number of children who came by car?

A 6

B 3

C 40

D 42

6 This line graph shows the temperature during one day.

What is the difference between the highest and lowest temperature in the day?

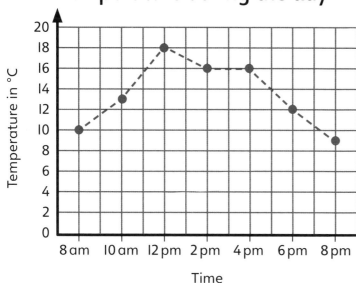

Temperature during the day

Temperature in °C / Time

→ **Practice book 4C p111**

Unit 16
Geometry – position and direction

In this unit we will …

⚡ Use numbers to say where things are on a grid

⚡ Plot points on a grid

⚡ Use our knowledge of shapes to complete diagrams

⚡ Describe translations on a grid

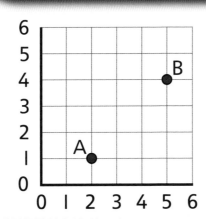

Point A is '2 across and I up'. Where is Point B?

We will need some maths words. Do you know what they mean?

position　　horizontal　　vertical

up　　down　　left　　right

coordinate　　plot　　vertex

vertices　　point　　grid

translate

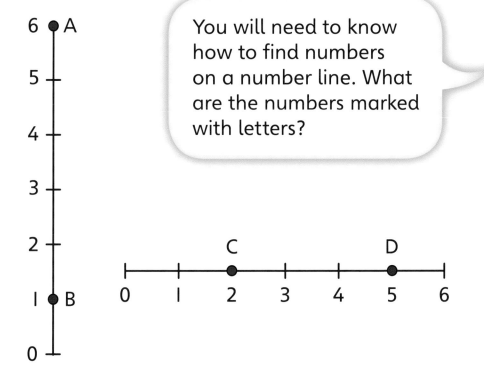

You will need to know how to find numbers on a number line. What are the numbers marked with letters?

Describe position

Discover

I am looking for the place that is next to the log flume, and close to a playground.

Bella

1 **a)** Which place is Bella looking for?
How can you tell?

b) Describe the position of the same place in another way.

Share

a) The roller coaster, the picnic spot and the ice cream shop are all next to the log flume.

I used both pieces of information. Only one place is next to the log flume **and** close to a playground.

Bella is looking for the roller coaster.

b) The position of the roller coaster can be described in lots of different ways.

I said that the roller coaster is between the playground and the lake.

I said that the roller coaster is beside the dropzone ride.

The roller coaster is half-way between the log flume and the dropzone ride.

Think together

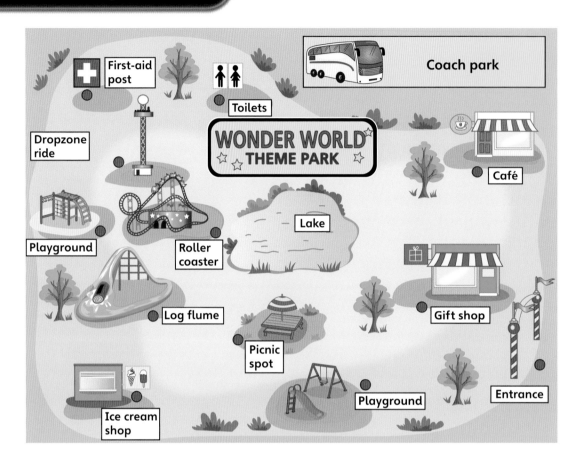

1   Identify each of these places from its description.

   a) The place near the top of the map, close to the coach park.

   b) The feature in the centre of the map.

   c) The closest place to the entrance.

   d) The closest place to the lake.

2   Describe the positions of these places. There may be more than one way to describe each one.

   a) The ice cream shop

   b) The café

   c) The dropzone ride

   d) The first-aid post

3 Here is another version of the map of the theme park.

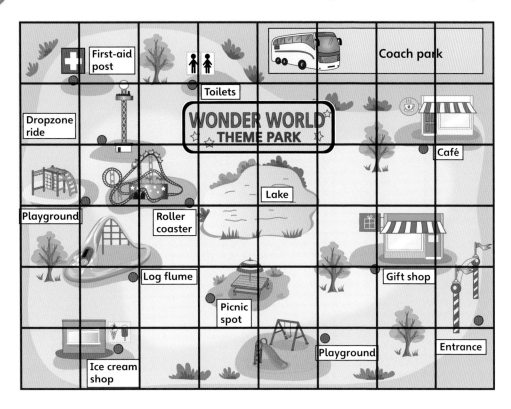

Use this version of the map to find each of these places from its description.

a) This place is half-way between the roller coaster and the ice cream shop.

b) This place is two spaces to the right of the first-aid post.

c) This place is seven spaces across from the left edge of the map, and three spaces up from the bottom.

Do the squares on the map (the **grid**) make it easier to describe where things are? Why?

159

Describe position using coordinates

Discover

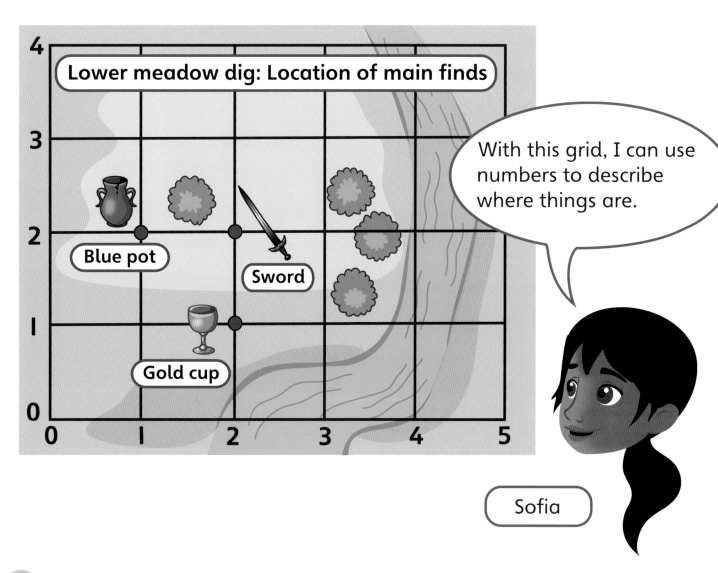

Lower meadow dig: Location of main finds

Blue pot

Sword

Gold cup

With this grid, I can use numbers to describe where things are.

Sofia

1 **a)** Which object was found at position (2,2)?

   b) What was found at position (2,1)?

Share

a)

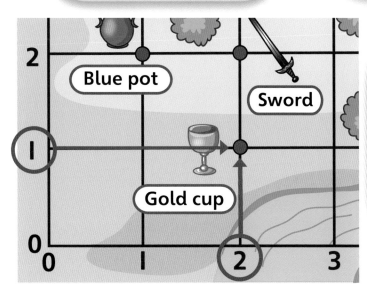

The sword was found at position (2,2).

b)

I think the blue pot is at (2,1), as it is 2 up and 1 across.

I think the gold cup is at (2,1) as it is 2 across and 1 up.

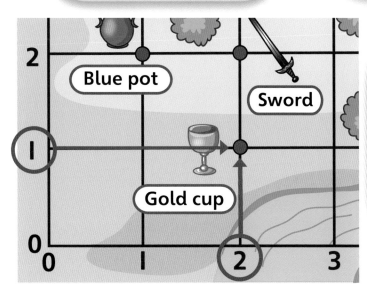

We always put the number across first, so (2,1) means 2 along and 1 up. (2,1) are called the **coordinates** of the **point**.

The gold cup was found at position (2,1).

161

Think together

1 Sofia marked the positions of some other objects on the map.

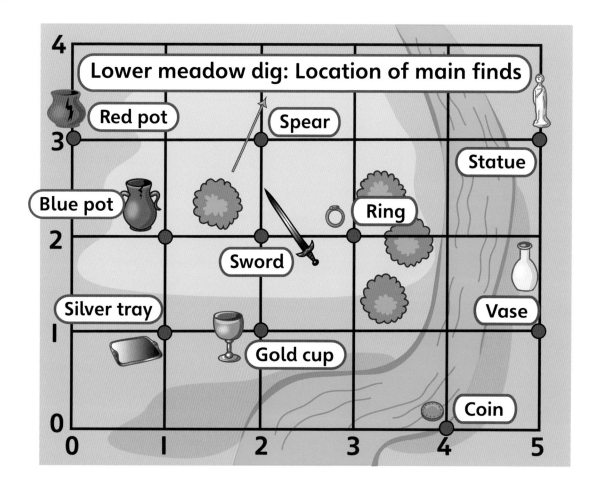

a) What is located at (1,2)?

b) What is located at (5,3)?

c) What is at the position with coordinates (2,3)?

162

2 Use the map from question I to answer these questions.

    a) What are the coordinates of the silver tray?

    b) Where were these objects found?

        i) The red pot

        ii) The coin

        iii) The vase

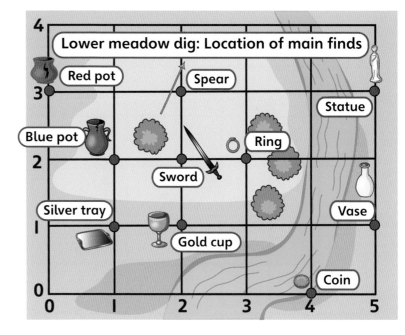

3 A dog walker found an old silver pin in the middle of the trees. Which of these could **not** be the position where the pin was found? Use the same map as in questions I and 2.

    A (2,2)

    B (3,2)

    C (4,1)

I need to remember to find the first coordinate along the horizontal line and the second coordinate upwards from there.

163

Plot coordinates

Discover

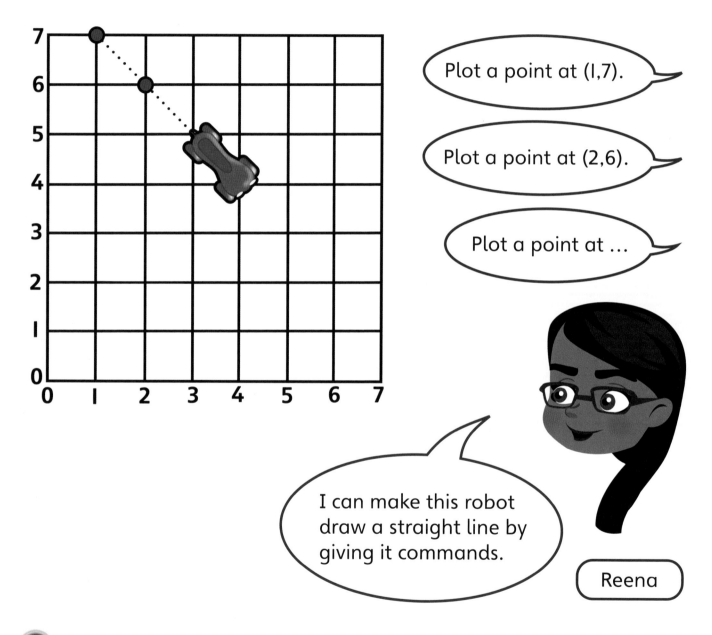

Plot a point at (1,7).

Plot a point at (2,6).

Plot a point at ...

I can make this robot draw a straight line by giving it commands.

Reena

1 **a)** What command did Reena use to plot the third dot?

b) What points should Reena plot to continue the dots in a straight line?

164

Share

a) The command Reena used to plot the third dot is: Plot a point at (3,5).

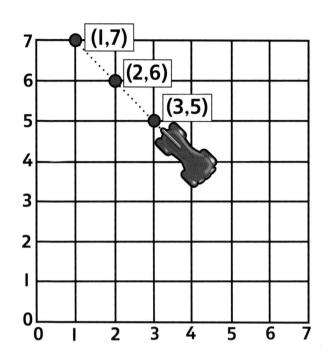

I started from 0. I counted across (horizontally), then up (vertically) to find the coordinates.

b)

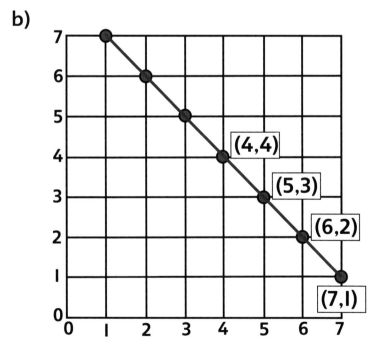

I drew a straight line through the dots to find the new points.

Reena should plot the points (4,4), (5,3), (6,2) and (7,1) to continue the dots in a straight line.

165

Think together

1 Plot these points on a grid.

What pattern do the points make?

(5,7)

(4,6)

(3,5)

(2,4)

(1,3)

(0,2)

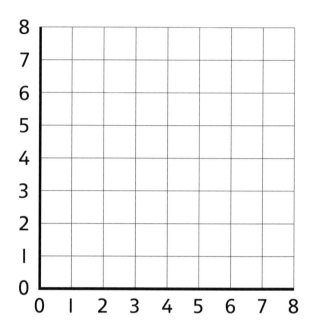

2 **a)** What are the coordinates of these points?

b) Plot the points on a grid that continue the same line.

List their coordinates.

c) Look at the list of coordinates. Could you have predicted what they were without plotting all the points?

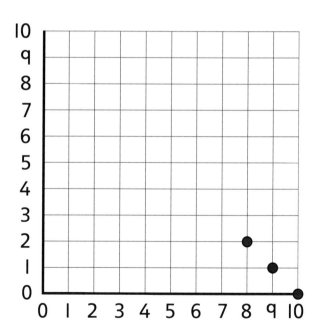

3 Emma used a robot to plot the points on the outline of a capital 'E'.

Plot a point at (0,4).

Plot a point at (3,4).

Emma

What were the rest of the commands that she used?

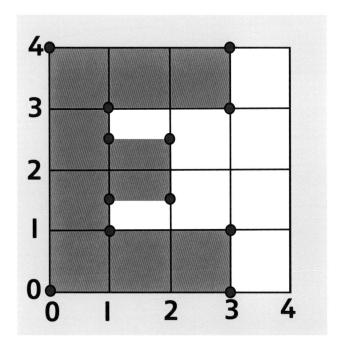

I can see that some of the coordinates are not whole numbers. I will need to use fractions.

167

→ Practice book 4C p120

Draw 2D shapes on a grid

Discover

Start at (1,4).

Draw a line to (1,1).

Draw a line to (4,1).

I can make this robot draw lines to make a square.

Richard

1 a) What command should Richard give next?

b) What is the final command that is needed to finish the square?

Share

a)

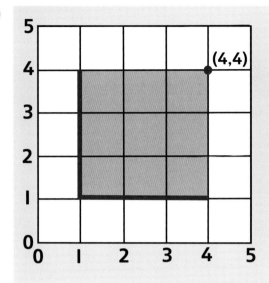 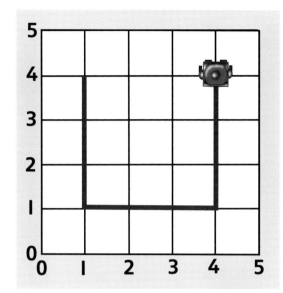

The next command Richard should give is:
Draw a line to (4,4).

I shaded the square to find where the missing corner was.

b)

A square has four sides, so you need to go back to the starting point to finish it.

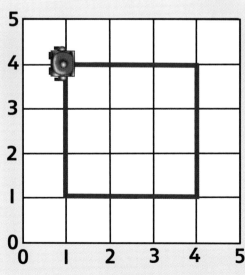

The final command that is needed to finish the square is: Draw a line to (1,4).

Think together

1 Zeb has plotted points at three of the corners of a rectangle.

What are the coordinates of the final corner?

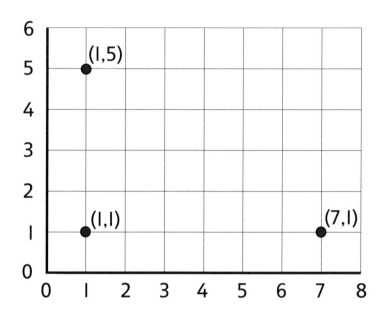

2 The two points on this grid are two corners of a square. The whole square fits inside the grid.

What are the coordinates of the other two corners?

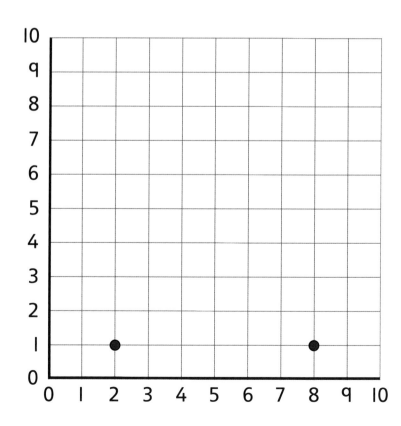

3 The two points on this grid are two corners of a square.

What are the coordinates of the other two corners?

There is more than one answer.

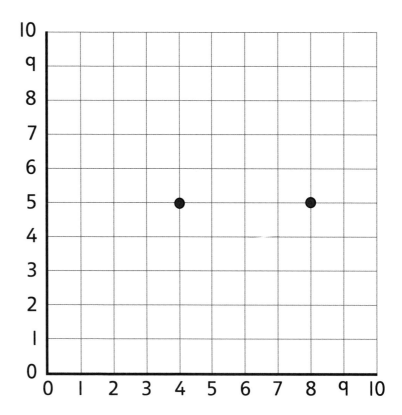

4 The coloured shape is part of a shape with one line of symmetry.

What are the missing coordinates of the **vertices** of the shape?

CHALLENGE

I can remember how to do this. Each vertex is the same distance on the other side of the line of symmetry.

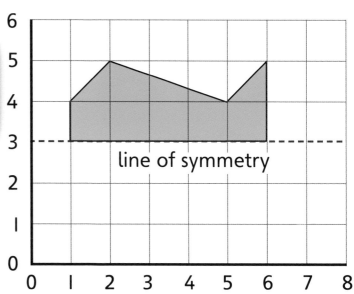
line of symmetry

171

→ Practice book 4C p123

Translate on a grid

Discover

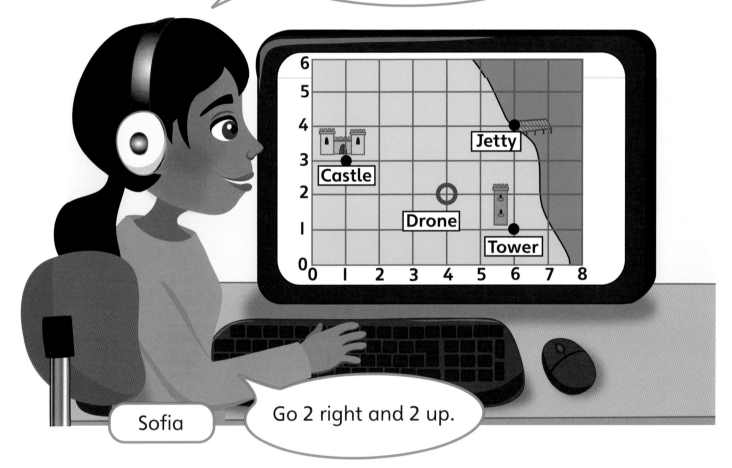

I am exploring a new site with a drone. There is something else I want to have a look at.

Go 2 right and 2 up.

Sofia

Translation is moving up or down, or side-to-side on a grid.

1 a) What feature does Sofia want to look at?

b) Later, the drone was at the tower and Sofia told it to move 5 left and 2 up. Where did she send the drone to?

Share

a) Sofia wants to look at the jetty.

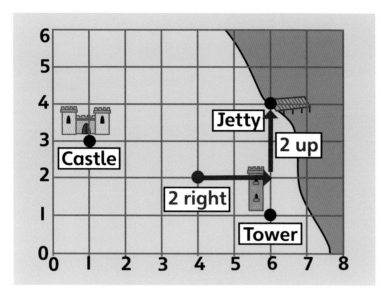

I drew the lines on the grid to show the drone going 2 right and 2 up.

b) The drone starts at the tower for this translation.

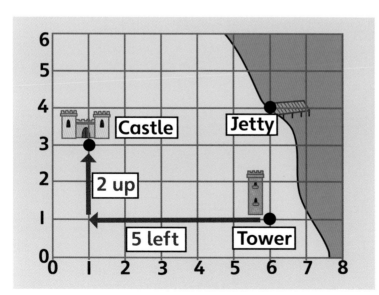

I wonder whether I could have worked out where the drone would go without drawing on the map.

Sofia sent the drone to the castle.

Think together

1 These commands will take the drone to all of the places marked on the map in turn.

In what order will the drone visit the places?

I left, 3 up

4 right, 3 down

I left, 3 up

4 down

5 left, 2 up

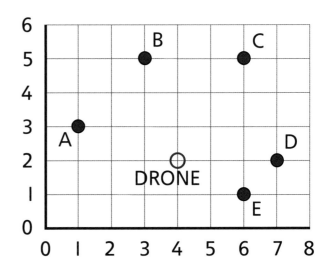

2 The map shows the position of three towns.

The translation from P to Q is '3 right, I up'. What translations do these instructions describe?

3 left, I down

4 right, 3 down

4 left, 3 up

I left, 4 up

I right, 4 down

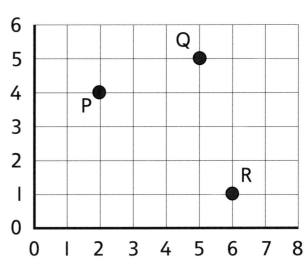

3 The rectangle slides across the grid so that corner A moves from (1,1) to (7,4).

Where do the three other corners of the rectangle move to?

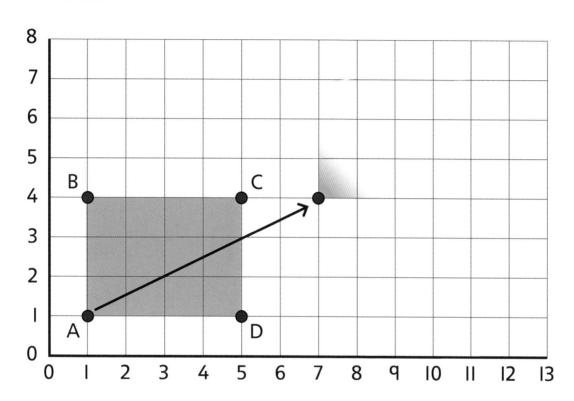

I will work out where each corner has moved to in turn.

I think there is another way. I will try to draw the rectangle in its new position.

175

Describe translation on a grid

Discover

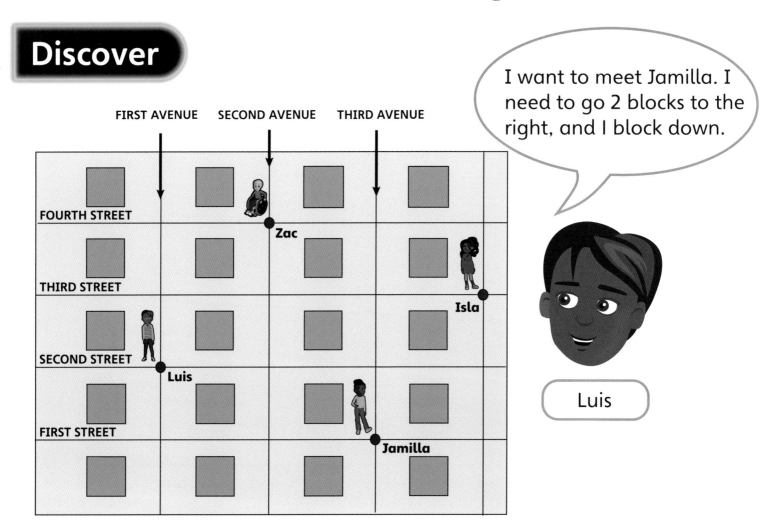

I want to meet Jamilla. I need to go 2 blocks to the right, and I block down.

Luis

1 a) Luis could describe his journey to Jamilla as '2 right, I down'.

If Jamilla went to Luis instead, how could she describe her journey?

b) Zac wants to meet Isla. He is not sure which of these is the correct journey:

- 2 right and then I down

- I down and then 2 right.

Which is correct?

Share

a)

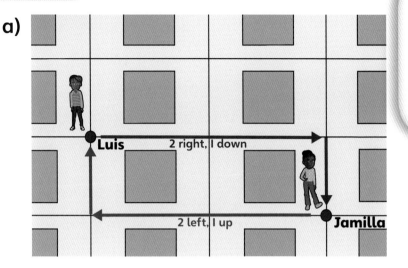

I think that Jamilla's journey is in the opposite direction to Luis's. So she will go left instead of right, and up instead of down.

Jamilla could write her journey as '2 left, I up'.

b)

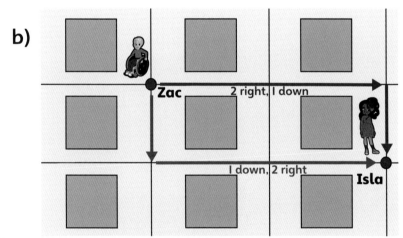

I drew both journeys on the grid to see where Zac finishes.

I learnt that it is the same journey whether you go right or go down first.

The journeys are the same: both are correct.

Think together

1 The four friends decide that they will all meet at a café at the point marked with an X.

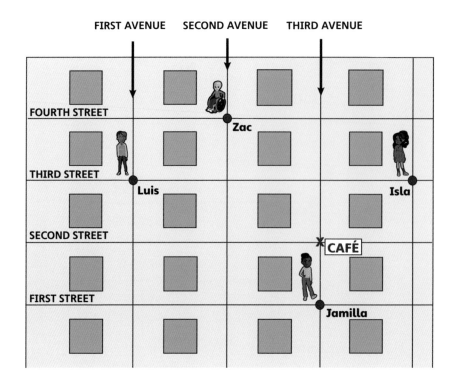

a) Describe Zac's journey.

b)

Isla: My journey is I left, I down.

Zac: I think your journey is I down, I left.

Who is right? Explain your answer.

c) Describe Luis's journey in two ways.

d) Describe Jamilla's journey.

2 The translation from A to B can be described as '5 left, 2 up'.

Describe the other translations.

A to B: 5 left, 2 up   B to A

A to C   C to A

B to C   C to B

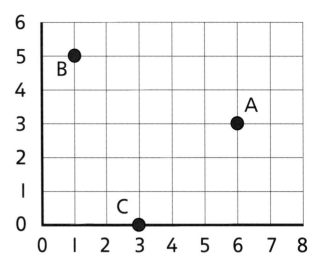

3 Describe these translations.

a) The blue rectangle translates to rectangle A.

b) The blue rectangle translates to rectangle B.

c) The blue rectangle translates to rectangle C.

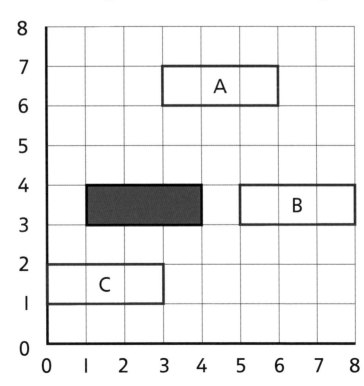

→ Practice book 4C p129

End of unit check

1 Which point has been plotted in the wrong position?

A Point Q

B Point R

C Point S

D Point T

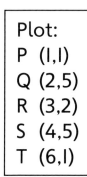

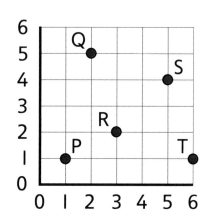

Plot:
P (1,1)
Q (2,5)
R (3,2)
S (4,5)
T (6,1)

2 Points E and F are two of the corners of a square.

Which of these points could not be another corner of the same square?

A Point A

B Point B

C Point C

D Point D

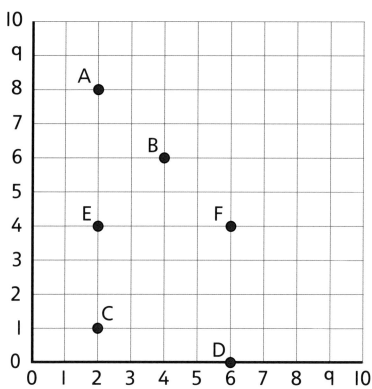

Use this grid for questions 3 to 5.

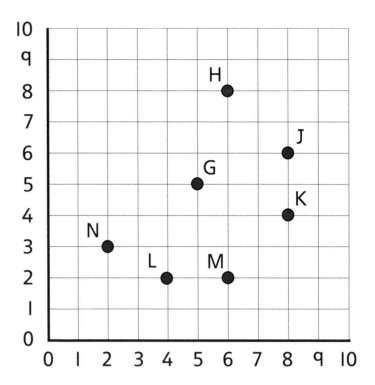

3 Which point would these instructions take you to?

Start at point G. Move 3 right, I down.

A Point J

B Point K

C Point H

D Point M

4 Which instructions describe the translation from G to N?

A 4 left, 3 down

B 3 left, 2 down

C 3 left, 4 down

D 2 left, 3 down

5 The translation 'I left, 3 down' finished at point G. Where did it start?

A Point H

B Point J

C Point L

D Point M

6 Draw the quadrilateral with vertices at (4,8), (7,5), (7,0) and (2,5) on a grid.

Which point could you move to change the quadrilateral to a square? What are the coordinates of the new point?

→ **Practice book 4C p132**

I enjoyed solving maths puzzles.

What have we learnt?

Can you do all these things?

⚡ Order and partition decimals
⚡ Convert and compare amounts of money
⚡ Recognise years, months and days
⚡ Compare and order angles
⚡ Interpret line graphs
⚡ Translate shapes on a grid

Remember, mistakes help us learn!

Now you are ready for the next books!

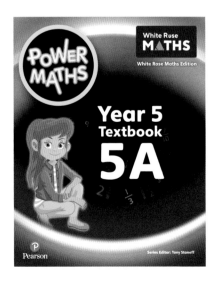

POWER MATHS

White Rose MATHS
White Rose Maths Edition

Year 5
Textbook
5A

Pearson

Series Editor: Tony Staneff

POWER MATHS

White Rose MATHS
White Rose Maths Edition

Year 5
Practice Book
5A

Pearson

Series Editor: Tony Staneff

Published by Pearson Education Limited, 80 Strand, London, WC2R 0RL.

www.pearsonschools.co.uk

Text © Pearson Education Limited 2018, 2023
Edited by Pearson and Florence Production Ltd
First edition edited by Pearson, Little Grey Cells Publishing Services and Haremi Ltd
Designed and typeset by Pearson and PDQ Digital Media Solutions Ltd
First edition designed and typeset by Kamae Design
Original illustrations © Pearson Education Limited 2018, 2023
Illustrated by Laura Arias, John Batten, Fran and David Brylewski, Diego Diaz, Nigel Dobbyn, Virginia Fontanabona, Adam Linley and Nadene Naude at Beehive Illustration; Emily Skinner at Graham-Cameron Illustration; and Kamae Design
Images: The Royal Mint, 1971, 1982, 1990, 1992, 1998, 2017, 2023: 38, 40–48, 50–52, 54, 56, 58, 60–62, 64; Bank of England: 38, 41, 43, 45, 47–49, 51, 53, 55, 57, 59, 61, 63, 65
Cover design by Pearson Education Ltd
Front and back cover illustrations by Diego Diaz and Nadene Naude at Beehive Illustration

Series editor: Tony Staneff
Lead author: Josh Lury
Consultants (first edition): Professor Liu Jian and Professor Zhang Dan

The rights of Tony Staneff and Josh Lury to be identified as authors of this work have been asserted by them in accordance with the Copyright, Designs and Patents Act 1988.

First published 2018
This edition first published 2023

27 26 25 24 23
10 9 8 7 6 5 4 3 2

British Library Cataloguing in Publication Data
A catalogue record for this book is available from the British Library

ISBN 978 1 292 41956 5

Printed in the UK by Bell & Bain Ltd, Glasgow

For Power Maths resources go to
www.activelearnprimary.co.uk

Note from the publisher
Pearson has robust editorial processes, including answer and fact checks, to ensure the accuracy of the content in this publication, and every effort is made to ensure this publication is free of errors. We are, however, only human, and occasionally errors do occur. Pearson is not liable for any misunderstandings that arise as a result of errors in this publication, but it is our priority to ensure that the content is accurate. If you spot an error, please do contact us at resourcescorrections@pearson.com so we can make sure it is corrected.